28531

D0426474

GOD
STILL
SPEAKS

GOD STILL SPEAKS

A Biblical View of
Christian Communication

Robert E. Webber
Professor of Theology
Wheaton College

Thomas Nelson Publishers
Nashville

Library of Congress Cataloging in Publication Data

Webber, Robert.
  God still speaks.

  Bibliography: p. 209
  1. Communication (Theology)   I. Title.
BV4319.W38   230'.01'41   80–53
ISBN 0–8407–5189–3

TO JOANNE

in appreciation for the
life we share together

CONTENTS

ACKNOWLEDGMENTS

It is exceedingly difficult to acknowledge everyone who in one way or another contributes to the writing of a book.

In general I want to recognize the Christian academic community. Since the beginning of my writing days I have found immeasurable support and help from Christian scholars.

I once heard Francis Schaeffer make a comment to the effect that the ultimate basis of communication is found in the Holy Trinity. This comment stuck with me, and occasionally I mulled it over in my mind, "playing" with the idea.

A few years later when the topic of communication began to be bantered about somewhat seriously in Christian circles, I decided to try to rough out the stray thoughts in my mind and to tie a few loose ends together. The result was a very short paper that I shared with James Johnson of the Wheaton Graduate School. He liked it and subsequently published it in *Spectrum*, the magazine of the Graham Center of Communications. The article caught the eye of James Engel, director of the Graduate School of Communications. He promptly asked me to develop a course on the subject and to write this book for the series he was editing for Thomas Nelson Publishers.

In particular, then, my appreciation is extended to Dr. Engel for suggesting this work. I also want to thank Arthur Holmes, Bishop Ronald Roberson, Peter Brooks, and Mark Fackler for their penetrating evaluations and helpful suggestions.

I am also indebted to my student, Matt Hussey, for combing the library for articles and books. The hours of typing by Amy Richards and Karen Mason have not gone unnoticed. Finally, I wish to thank Amy for her painstaking work on the index.

GOD
STILL
SPEAKS

GOD STILL SPEAKS:
AN INTRODUCTION

A Christian view of communication centers around the conviction that *God still speaks*. That phrase, however, implies something else—namely that God has spoken.[1]

Thinking people have always asked the BIG questions: Where did what exists come from? Who am I? What is the *meaning* of my life? Is there life after death? Is man accountable to a higher being?

Christians believe that God has spoken to these questions. The answers are found in the Scriptures of the Old and New Testaments, which together preserve the canonical record of much of God's communications to man. If we want to know God's Word regarding the major issues of life, we must turn to the Holy Scriptures as our only infallible guide.

Although various branches of Christendom may disagree on the interpretations of various passages of Scripture, there is a clearly discernible common faith that all true Christians share. That faith is expressed, for example, in the Nicene Creed, which is a summary of scriptural teaching. The significance of this creed for the Christian is that it sets forth the framework of the Christian world-view—namely the teaching about God, creation, incarnation, redemption, the church, and the consummation of all things.

The Nicene Creed was originally written in A.D. 325 by an ecumenical council of the church. It was discussed until A.D. 381, when it was finally adopted by the entire church as an adequate

---

[1]For a good introduction to modern views on revelation, see John Baillie, *The Idea of Revelation in Recent Thought* (New York: Columbia University Press, 1956).

13

and truthful statement of Christian teaching. Since then, the Nicene Creed has been accepted by the whole believing church.[2]

THE NICENE CREED

We believe in one God,
    the Father, the Almighty,
    maker of heaven and earth,
    of all that is, seen and unseen.

We believe in one Lord, Jesus Christ,
    the only Son of God,
    eternally begotten of the Father,
    God from God, Light from Light,
    true God from true God,
    begotten, not made,
    of one substance with the Father.
    Through Him all things were made.
    For us and for our salvation
      He came down from heaven;
    by the power of the Holy Spirit
      He became incarnate from the Virgin Mary,
      and was made man.
    For our sake He was crucified under Pontius Pilate;
      He suffered death and was buried.
      On the third day He rose again
        in accordance with the Scriptures;
      He ascended into heaven
        and is seated at the right hand of the Father.
    He will come again in glory to judge the living
      and the dead,
    and His kingdom will have no end.

We believe in the Holy Spirit, the Lord, the giver
    of life,
    who proceeds from the Father.
    With the Father and the Son He is worshiped and
      glorified.
    He has spoken through the prophets.

---

[2]For a good introduction to the history of the Nicene Creed, see J.N.D. Kelly, *Ea Christian Creeds* (New York: David McKay Co., 1972), 3rd ed.

We believe in one holy catholic and apostolic church.
We acknowledge one baptism for the forgiveness of
  sins.
We look for the resurrection of the dead,
  and the life of the world to come. Amen.

COMMUNICATION AND
THE CHRISTIAN WORLD-VIEW

The purpose of this writing is not to set forth a case for the Christian world-view. It is instead *to describe a view of communication from the context of the Christian world-view.*

First, this means that Christianity as the only viable world-view is the presupposition of this work. The reader who shares this opinion will most readily benefit from my arguments and their implications for communciations. The reader who does not now accept the Christian world-view may find himself wanting to test the Christian framework.[3]

Secondly, because the nature of this work is to describe a Christian view of communication, I will not enter into an apologetic dialogue with approaches to communication based on other world-views. I am keenly aware that the faith-commitment one makes—whether to empiricism, Marxism, phenomenology, mysticism, or Christianity—determines the outcome of one's thought. *But the purpose of this work is description not dialogue.*

There is no neutral and unbiased view of communication. All interpretations of communication are to one extent or another determined by the assumptions of the interpreter. A major assumption behind the Christian view of communication is that *God has spoken* and that *God still speaks.*

To say that God still speaks means several things. I do not mean to suggest that God is revealing new truth today. The church has always and everywhere confessed that the doctrine God has revealed in the Scripture is sufficient—there is no need for additional revelation.

Rather, the idea that God still speaks must be understood in

---

[3]A good brief modern apologetic for the Christian faith is Nicholas Wolterstorff, *Reason Within the Bounds of Religion* (Grand Rapids: Eerdmans, 1976).

the context of a dynamic view of life. That is, there is an ongoing of God's communication. Otherwise God would no longer be active; the Holy Spirit would be static. What God has said continues to be said.[4] Therefore, in order to hear what God is saying today we must listen to what God has said already.

In the first place God has spoken and still speaks through His creation. The psalmist declares, "The heavens are *telling* of the glory of God . . ." (Ps. 19:1, italics mine). Creation, the Christian confesses, continues to proclaim its Creator. Therefore *the creation is a worthy vehicle through which God actively makes Himself known to us today.*

Secondly, God has spoken in Scripture. What God has said to man in the context of his history from Adam to the close of the apostolic age has been gathered in a Book. This Book is no ordinary book, for it contains the authentic and authoritative writings of those who heard the Word of God and wrote it down. It records not only what God said to man, but how God came to man in the Person of Jesus Christ, the Son of God. *The Scripture continues to speak today because it is the written source of God's communication to man.*

Thirdly, God has created the church as the context in which His communication to man is preserved, interpreted, and passed on. *The church is therefore the living voice of God to the world.* Unless the church speaks, what God has said goes unheard.

To suggest then that God still speaks is to recognize the *vehicle* through which God speaks (the physical and material world); the *written source* of God's continuing communication (the Scripture); and the *voice* through which He communicates (the church). These elements are all necessary aspects of a Christian view of communication.

I have organized this writing around three concerns: (1) a call to effective communication, (2) a description of a biblical view of communication, and (3) some implications for contemporary communication.

---

[4]See Walter J. Ong, S.J., *The Presence of the Word* (New Haven: Yale University Press, 1967).

Chapters 1–3 deal with the first concern: a call to effective communication. In these chapters I will show the *need* for a theology of communication.

In Chapters 4–8, I will develop *a biblical view of communication* based on the Christian world-view.

Chapters 9–11 examine *the role of the church as communicator.*

Finally, in Chapter 12 I set forth thirteen principles for Christian communicators. These principles are basic to Christian communications and must be taken into account by all who want to effectively communicate God's Word today.

In the writing of this manuscript, I have made quite generous use of such words as *man* and *mankind* in their traditional, generic sense; these words are especially prevalent in Chapters 6 and 7. I want to assure my female readers that I have them in view when I use these traditional words.

My concern throughout the writing has been to bring the theoretical and practical together. I am convinced that to have one without the other is to travel a dead-end street.

The time for reflection has come. If we can think deeply and critically about Christian communications without losing the energy and zeal that is characteristic of the growing Christian communications empire, then we will have succeeded indeed.

I.
A CALL
TO EFFECTIVE
COMMUNICATION

1
THE GOSPEL
AND THE CULTURAL GRID

In the church of Jesus Christ there are certain axioms held by everyone. Some of these are *theological*, such as belief in the Trinity and the confession that Jesus is both fully human and fully divine. Others are of a more *practical* nature, such as the need for prayer or fellowship or service.

Like these, the calling of the church to *communicate* the gospel is a universally accepted axiom. The church always and everywhere recognizes that salvation is not something to hide, but rather to be passed on. In the words of Jesus, "you will be witnesses of Me . . . to the end of the earth" (Acts 1:8). For this reason one may define the task of the Christian church as *communicating Christ to the contemporary world*.[1]

To define the task of the church in this way raises two very basic questions: (1) Who is Christ? (2) What is the contemporary world? Although it may appear as an oversimplification to begin with such fundamental questions, it would be presumptuous to merely assume a consensus view. There are many views of Christ and a variety of attitudes toward the contemporary world.

WHO IS CHRIST?

No one would deny that the task of the Christian communicator is to introduce the Lord Jesus Christ to others. This was certainly the dominant concern of the apostles. The concern to preach the true Christ can be clearly seen in the sermons recorded in the opening chapters of Acts.

---

[1] I am using the word *task* in an inclusive way. Communicating Christ is not limited to evangelism. Rather, it is the calling of the church to demonstrate how Christ as the center of the universe is related to every aspect of the created order.

But who is this Christ whom we are called to communicate? To answer this question, I will discuss quite briefly *false christs, distorted christs,* and the biblical Christ.

False Christs

The church has always been confronted by heterodox views of Christ. Even during the New Testament times, false prophets and deceivers arose. For this reason Paul repeatedly had to warn against a preoccupation with "myths and endless genealogies, which give rise to mere speculation . . ." (1 Tim. 1:4), and John had to declare "who is the liar but the one who denies that Jesus is the Christ?" (1 John 2:22).

It is not an overgeneralization to say that most of the false views about Christ have overemphasized either His humanity or His divinity. This was true in the early decades of the church as Christians fought off the Gnostics, who made Christ some sort of divine "appearance," or the dynamic monarchists, who thought Jesus was little more than a mere man who received the Spirit and was later adopted into the Godhead as a "reward" for His good life and death.

The same sort of problems face us today. The false views held about Christ tend to so humanize Him that we no longer have a divine Jesus, or they tend to so divinize Him that we no longer have a human Jesus.

For example, the liberal view that Jesus is "just a good man" certainly falls into this former category. This view results from the nineteenth-century quest for the historical Jesus. This quest labored under the assumption that there was a difference between the gospel *of* Jesus and the gospel *about* Jesus. The gospel about Jesus, these early liberals told us, was the gospel *created* by the disciples. *They* had made Jesus into a god—a metaphysical creature, a supernatural being. Liberals argued that it was at this point that all theology went wrong. Their evidence was this: A closer look at the teachings of Jesus, they said, demonstrate Him to be only another man—a good man, a man of unique insight, a man who reflected God. Thus the task of the Christian communicator, they said, was to strip the New Testament of all its supernatural baggage (which no modern man can really accept, they reasoned) and get back to the "simple" teachings of Jesus. Consequently, Christianity was reduced to the message of "love"—love God and your neighbor and all will be well.[2]

Others who sought the historical Jesus concluded that we could only find the Jesus of faith. This is the Jesus that lives in the hearts of a community called after His name. Where the notion of Jesus came from or how it got there, they alleged, is relatively unimportant. The issue is that the church has *experienced* Jesus. He meets their needs. Jesus is reduced to a religious idea that meets the hungers of man. The conclusion is that we can have the Easter faith without the Easter fact. The *effect* of Jesus in our lives, according to those who hold this view, is all that matters.[3]

Both of these notions about Christ are judged as false by the true church because they deny that Jesus Christ is truly God and truly Man. These views are relatively easy to discern, refute, and reject because they are so clearly out of harmony with the consistent historic, biblical confession of the church.

Distorted Christs

It is more difficult and more controversial to discuss views about Christ that are somewhat less distorted. The reason I say this is because I want to argue that all of us have, in one way or another, a distorted view of Christ.[4] By this I mean to say that no one person or Christian group has a view of Christ that is entirely free from some kind of cultural or philosophical grid. I am not making the church the culprit for this situation. Indeed the mere recognition of it is little more than the willingness to accept the fact that we always do our theological thinking through an inescapable grid. To recognize this situation is to acknowledge that we hold these truths in earthen vessels (see 2 Cor. 4:7).

Although there are probably as many grids as there are cultures in the world, it will be sufficient to mention three: the Western Christ, the Eastern Christ, and the Third-World

---

[2]See Adolf Harnack, *What Is Christianity?* (New York: Harper & Row, 1957).

[3]See Albert Schweitzer, *The Quest of the Historical Jesus* (New York: Macmillan, 1953).

[4]See John R. W. Stott, *Christ the Controversialist* (Downers Grove, Ill.: Inter-Varsity Press, 1970), and J. B. Phillips, *Your God Is Too Small* (New York: Macmillan, 1953).

Christ. I do not intend to be exhaustive. I only want to demonstrate the principle—namely that we have different ways of talking about the same Christ. The illustrations used will be more in keeping with the popular notion rather than any official church view.

In the West many of us believe in a white, Anglo-Saxon, middle-class Christ. Christ is rational, cultured, nice, and polite. He is the popular Jesus whom everyone likes. He's always ready with a helping hand. He's warm and friendly, outgoing and kind. When you need a friend, Jesus is near. He's always doing nice things for you. He can give you a flashy car, a large home, and lots of other beautiful things if you only believe and serve Him. It's an exchange. You give Him your life, and He will give you peace, happiness, contentment, and maybe even make you rich, successful, and popular.[5]

The East has somewhat modeled its Christ after a mystical, poetical image. Jesus is somewhat remote from experience. He's the Baby in the virgin's arms or the Judge of all creation who is pictured in icons and frescoes of the church. He is always dressed in robes and fine linen. There is a halo around His head; He is always surrounded by worshipers. Those who do get close to Jesus do so especially out of a commitment to some kind of ascetic or monastic life. They cannot engage in the normal affairs of raising a family or running a business because it takes a lot of time and concentrated effort to get to know Jesus.[6]

In *the Third World* Christ looks like a revolutionary. He wears tattered clothes and identifies with the poor. You will always find Him among those who are suffering under the bondage of the rich, and He is always ready to lead the poor out of their misery. He may be carrying a picket sign, agitating for structural change in the society, or leading a pack of guerillas. Wherever He is, He's in the midst of a struggle—fighting for human rights, the dignity of every man, the final release from all misery.[7]

[5]For an example of this view see Bruce Barton, *The Man Nobody Knows* (Indianapolis: The Bobbs-Merrill Co., Charter Books, 1962).
[6]See John Meyendorff, *St. Gregory Palamas and Orthodox Spirituality* (New York: St. Vladimir Seminary Press, 1974).
[7]See Gustav Guiteren, *Theology of Liberation* (Mary Knoll, N.Y.: Oribs Books, 1974).

Now admittedly I've painted three somewhat exaggerated pictures. But I have done so to illustrate that Christ is pictured differently, depending on the cultural milieu. Nevertheless, I would also argue that behind each of these portraits is the biblical Christ; at the very least those who hold each view have tried to fit the biblical Christ into their cultural situation.

In and of itself, this is not wrong. However it becomes wrong when the picture of Christ is confused with the biblical Jesus. When *our* interpretation of Christ is made *essential*, then the true biblical Christ automatically becomes secondary. This problem is central to the question of communication.

Who is it that we communicate when we preach Christ? Do we end up communicating a Western, Eastern, Third World, or another somewhat distorted and secondary interpretation of Christ? Or, are we able to separate our cultural Christ from the biblical Christ? We must learn to let go of a lot of cultural baggage in order for the biblical Christ to be seen more clearly. But who is this biblical Christ?

The Biblical Christ

If the task of the Christian church is to *communicate* the biblical Christ, then we ought to *know* the biblical Christ. Space does not permit an exhaustive examination of this subject, so I will be selective and limit myself to two biblical images of Christ that are often overlooked by modern Christians. These are the images of (1) the *Second Adam* and (2) the *cosmic Christ*.

The image of Christ as the Second Adam is found in several passages of the New Testament, but the most striking use of this figure is set forth in Romans 5:12–21. We may put this passage into the setting of three images of man: original man, fallen man, redeemed man.* Think of two ladders placed up against a wall with twenty or thirty feet between them; original man is on the ladder to the left. He is the first Adam. It doesn't matter how long he has been there. What matters is the relationship he sustains with God, himself, his neighbor, and nature. He is in harmony with the whole universe. There is no alienation or separation

---

*The use of the words *man* and *mankind* refer to all humanity and are not meant to exclude women. See the Introduction for further explanation.

within him. He is a whole person who is able to commune with God.

This first Adam has the power of choice. He may choose to commune with God or choose not to. His choice is to go his own way. He wants to be independent, to be free, to create his own life. Consequently he goes down the ladder away from God. His choice is a movement away from what he has enjoyed in communion with God.

So man is now described as fallen. He is on the ground (to use our image), separated and alienated from the reality he enjoyed in union with God and the created order. Now the world and all that is in it gradually become objects to him. They are outside of him. Thus even the creation is affected; the ground is cursed and feels its separation from man and the effects of man's separation. The integral nature of life and reality is undergoing a breakdown. The cosmos is torn now by greed, strife, hate, violence, passion, and a host of other evil energies. It is ruled by these powers, these hosts of wickedness, these rulers of darkness. And the whole earth groans along with man, because the separations that have occurred throughout the cosmos cause severe pain. Paul describes the effect of this fall with words that touch down deeply into the midst of life—*sin*, *death*, and *condemnation*.

How can man and his world be put back together again? No mere man can do it, for all men are caught in the quagmire of their own undoing. Only God can save. But since it was a man's choice to move away from God, it took another Man, and His choice to move toward God, to bring life and the created order back together again. This Man is Christ, the God-Man, who through His incarnation, death, and resurrection *reverses* what the first Adam did and *restores* man and the creation. Christ, the Second Adam, through the power of his death and resurrection brings believing man and the creation up that second ladder and makes all things new.

Irenaeus, an early church father, spoke of this as a *recapitulation*, which means to "do it over again." The image of Christ as Second Adam is just that: He did it over again. The first Adam did something *to* the human race and creation: He initiated its destruction. The Second Adam did something *for* the human race and creation: He initiated and will ultimately accomplish its re-creation.

The second image, the *cosmic Christ*, is integral to Christ's image as the Second Adam and to the idea of the recapitulation of all things in Him. A summary of this notion is found in Colossians 1:15–19:

> He is the image of the invisible God, the firstborn over all creation. For by Him all things were created that are in heaven and that are on earth, visible and invisible, whether thrones or dominions or principalities or powers. All things were created by Him and for Him. And He is before all things, and in Him all things hold together. And He is the head of the body, the church, who is the beginning, the firstborn from the dead, that in all things He may have the preeminence. For it pleased the Father that in Him all fullness should dwell. . . .

Here Paul was expounding a belief about Christ that apparently was basic to the apostolic understanding of Jesus. We know from Genesis 1:26 that all men are made in the image of God. But Jesus, the Second Adam, is the *perfect image of God*—the perfect and complete Man.

He is also the *Creator*. As Paul wrote, ". . . by Him all things were created that are in heaven and that are on earth, visible and invisible, whether thrones or dominions or principalities or powers. All things were created by Him and for Him." As though this were not enough, Paul went on to state an absolutely incomprehensible idea about Jesus, namely that "in Him all things hold together." Whatever it is that gives meaning, consistency, unity, and energy to the universe—to the entire created order—it comes from Jesus. An illustration of the relationship of the cosmic order to Christ is drawn from the church. Christ is the Head; the church is the body.

But the capstone of the biblical description of the cosmic Christ is Paul's unprecedented persuasion that this One in whom all things consist is also the *Reconciler* of all things. For God has through Him reconciled "all things . . . whether things on earth or things in heaven, having made peace through the blood of His cross."

Thus the reconciliation brought by the Second Adam is cosmic. It affects not only man but also the entire created order. The sin-caused breakdown of communication within the created order, which produced alienation, separation, and division, is now being healed. No wonder Paul was able to write to the Romans of the coming glory of creation. Creation, he wrote, "eagerly waits for the revealing of the sons of God . . . because the creation itself also will be delivered from the bondage of corruption into the glorious liberty of the children of God" (Rom. 8:19,21).

As we preach and communicate Christ, we ought not to have a vision less than that given through the rich images of Christ as the Second Adam and the Cosmic Figure. To be sure, these images do not fully describe the biblical Christ, but they are central to our understanding of Him. Christ must never be made less than what these images imply; if He is, the biblical Christ is not being preached and communicated.

THE NATURE OF THE CONTEMPORARY WORLD

If the task of the church is to communicate Christ and if, as I have argued, it is important to have a handle on *what* we are communicating, then it is equally important to know something about the ones to whom we are communicating.

Unfortunately there are some who are so interested in understanding the gospel that they never take time to understand the context into which this gospel is preached. And there are those who are so concerned with understanding the world to which they are communicating that they fail to get a good grasp on the gospel.) John Stott speaks eloquently to this polarization in the following words:

We evangelicals love Scripture. We believe in biblical inspiration and authority. We find our hearts set on fire within us as Christ opens to us the Scriptures. We love to study this book. But as we expound the Scripture, we tend to leave it up in the air. We don't earth it in the contemporary world. On the other hand (although I know that I am oversimplifying it), the more liberal Christians study the contemporary world. They understand the contemporary world. They live in the contemporary world. They are modern

men and women. They read the paperbacks. They read the under-
ground press. They go to movies. They watch television. They look
at the world's art. They read the world's poetry. They understand
the contemporary world. But they have lost their grasp of the
historic biblical gospel. And so you have another tragic polarization: on the one hand, evangelicals who live in Scripture but who
don't earth it in the contemporary world, and on the other, radicals
who live in the contemporary world but have no biblical gospel to
relate to it.[8]

Assuming the general notion of "understanding the world" as a
necessary prerequisite for good communication, I will set forth
three characteristics of the contemporary world that effective
communicators must keep in mind. (1) There is great diversity in
the contemporary world. (2) Each culture has its own world-
view. (3) Communicating to the contemporary world is not as
simple as it may seem.

Diversity in the Contemporary World

The complexity of human communication becomes apparent as
we study the wide variety of world-views that exist today. In the
plurality of the Western world, for example, people with differing world-views may be neighbors. Even within groups of people
who have much in common there may be numerous ways of
perceiving reality.

Thus, communication of the gospel cannot be the same at all
times and under all conditions. This does not mean that the
content of the gospel must change. Absolutely not! But the
method of proclaiming the gospel, if it is to be effectively communicated in various cultures, must be delivered in terms that
will be understood by the receiving culture. God speaks in many
different ways and through a rich variety of means. He does not
speak in a monotone!

Each Culture Has Its Own World-view

The second characteristic grows out of the first and recognizes

[8]John R.W. Stott, "Communicating the God Who Has Spoken," *World Vision* (Sept.,
1975), p. 19.

that our world of multi-cultures is characterized by many world-views. What is a world-view? It is really a way of thinking about the world, *a way of interpreting reality*. As such, it is conditioned by a multitude of factors—personal, cultural, social, geographical, historical, and philosophical. Robert Redfield defines a world-view as follows:

> "World-view" attends especially to the way a man, in a particular society, sees himself in relation to all else. It is the properties of existence as distinguished from and related to the self. It is, in short, a man's idea of the universe. It is that organization of ideas that answers to a man with the questions: "Where am I? Among what do I move? What are my relations to these things?"[9]

A brief review of the history of the church will quickly persuade us that the gospel has again and again been contextualized into various world-views.

For example, the gospel originated within the Hebraic context. Its thought patterns and practices were therefore oriented around the Hebraic mind-set. A Hebraic world-view is integral, relational, and *holistic*. The biblical writers, for example, don't analyze or systematize. Their orientation is around history and historical events that give meaning to life. So it was with the early expression of the Christian faith. Christians worshiped God as Father, Son, and Holy Spirit. But they had no *systematic* view of the Trinity similar to that worked out by the First Council of Nicaea in 325. Likewise they confessed that Jesus was both of the flesh and of the Spirit. In this sense we can trace the common faith that Jesus is both human and divine back to the earliest faith of the church, but it certainly wasn't spelled out as it was later in the Chalcedonian Definition of 451.

As the faith moved into the Roman culture, it began to reflect the pragmatic orientation of the Roman world-view. Romans were known for their roads, aqueducts, and splendid architecture. This hard-nosed practical approach to life is seen in the

[9]Quoted by David Hesselgrave, *Communicating Christ Cross-Culturally* (Grand Rapids: Zondervan, 1978), p. 126.

developments within the Latin church. The Roman mind was organized, systematic, and pragmatic. So Roman Christianity reflected this in the practicality of its organization and in its emphasis on *practical living*. More than anything, though, the Romans gave the West the achievement of law. Their ability to make law and to practice government regulated by law gradually began to affect their theology. This was expanded into the necessity for satisfaction through penance and gradually developed into the merit system against which the Reformers rebelled.

We can see a similar cultural relationship in the East. The great contribution of the Greeks was in the area of the *aesthetic*. They gave Rome its poets. Their culture emphasized imagination, mystery, and philosophy. As Christianity invaded this culture, the Greek-Christian world-view took on some of these cultural characteristics. It was really the Greek Fathers who wrestled with the deepest philosophical issues of the Christian faith. How can God be one yet three? How can Jesus be human yet divine? They used their minds to grapple with the doctrinal areas of Scripture and to find ways of talking about these great mysteries and celebrating them in worship. They found a language that helped people understand what could not be easily understood. They developed a framework to speak about that which could not be readily systematized. They gave shape and form to classical Christianity—a way of thinking about truth that is still basic to all Christian theologizing.

Likewise in the West, since the time of the Reformation, Protestants have tried to relate the Christian message to changing world-views. When the Enlightenment propounded reason as the touchstone of reality, Protestants were quick to defend the Christian faith as a *reasonable* system of thought. When the Romantics stated that the heart is the center of man's being, the place where we intuit or experience truth, Christians were ready and willing to touch base at that point as well.

I don't mean to imply that all attempts to relate the gospel to differing world-views are equally successful. There is always the danger of syncretism on the one hand and accommodation on the other. Whenever and wherever Christian truth has been compromised or changed the method must be judged a failure. For then, Christian truth has not really been communicated. Rather, it has become somebody's idea of the truth, not the doctrine of the holy church.

Nevertheless the point is clear. The task of the Christian communicator is to communicate the biblical gospel to people of every culture.

The Complex Nature of Communicating Christ

The third characteristic we must keep in mind as Christian communicators is that communication is not a simple matter. Nevertheless, it is not so complex that we ought to despair. Even though recent studies undertaken at Yale University conclude that there are at least seventy-five common elements in all world-views, it is possible to break these down into several manageable groupings. According to Redfield there are three major ideas around which almost all aspects of a culture may be grouped, namely man, nature, and God (or supernature).[10] Since the Christian world-view may be grouped around these concerns also, we may recognize that there is already a built-in point of contact where we may begin to communicate.

Beyond this, however, it is not so simple. Thus, it is important for us to avoid two extremes: (1) the belief that communication is a matter of technique and (2) the belief that communication is simply a matter of proclaiming the gospel as we understand it.

The assumption that communication is a matter of technique is regarded by David Read as the "Western heresy." It assumes that through "psychological research, high-pressure advertising, opinion polls, mass-suggestion, success stories, modern business methods," and other technological manipulations people can be brought into the fold. Read puts his finger on the central problem when he writes:

> The Christian problem of communication is not to be solved merely by discerning what people want and giving them it. This is to

[10]Ibid, p. 128.

transform the gospel challenge of "Repent and believe" into a cynical technique of winning friends and influencing people.[11]

The message is lost when all concentration is on technique. Rather than proclaiming the Good News, we end up preaching moral do-goodism or selling a quick-and-easy "pill" to ward off evil.

On the other hand, however, we must avoid the opposite extreme of not giving any consideration to the people to whom we are communicating. The error in this direction is that we may not be communicating what we think we are communicating. We may understand what we are saying, but the receiver may not. Our listeners may have a set of presuppositions or a foreign cultural context that causes them to hear something quite different from what we are saying.

The matter of communication is not simple. We *must* proclaim the gospel; yet we must do this in such a way that the gospel, and not some distorted version of it, is heard.

CONCLUSION

In this chapter I have attempted to open up the question of communication by posing the question: What is the *task* of the Christian communicator? I have suggested that this task is to communicate Christ to the contemporary world.

We do not want to communicate an incorrect image of Christ. Therefore we must be very careful not to communicate an over-divinized Christ, a mere existential idea. We should also steer clear of a Jesus who is only human. Furthermore, we need to remember that we tend to interpret Christ through our own cultural grid. Our image of Him may be filtered through the grid of Western pragmatism, Eastern mysticism, or Third-World nationalism. We must put these distorted images behind us and return to the biblical image of Christ as the Second Adam, the

[11]David Haxton Carswell Read, *The Communication of the Gospel* (London: SCM Press, 1972), p.17.

Cosmic Figure who through His incarnation, death, and resurrection has destroyed the dominion of Satan and will put sin and
death under His feet at His second coming. To trust in Christ is to
enter into His kingdom and to look expectantly toward the future
in this hope.

The second side of our task is communicating the biblical Christ
to the *contemporary world*. This is not an easy task since there
are many cultures in the contemporary world, each one with its
own world-view. For this reason we must seek points of contact
while avoiding dependency upon techniques; neither should we
assume that proclamation of the message, with no consideration
of the cultural contexts and the world-views of the persons to
whom we speak, is sufficient.

This concern to communicate Christ cross-culturally should not
be seen as something new or revolutionary. Indeed it is a method
that goes back to the apostles. The original proclaimers of Christ
were not blind to cultural differences. They did not assume Christian teaching could make an automatic and simple transfer from
one culture to the next. Witness the struggle of the early church
as Christianity passed from the Hebraic community to the Hel-
lenistic community (see Acts 6 and 7). Consider the continuing
depth of thought and emotion that engulfed the early church as
they considered the inclusion of the Gentiles (see Acts 10, 11, 15,
21). Ponder the technique of Paul as he sought to communicate to
the Athenian skeptics (see Acts 17). Such tasks required intelligent thought and dependency upon the Holy Spirit.

In sum, we may conclude that the Scriptures supply us with the
data we want to communicate, and the current perspective
supplies us with the context through which this data must be
filtered. But the goal is not the communication of mere data; we
want the hearers of the gospel to experience the living God and
His saving action in Jesus Christ.

Having analyzed the task of Christian communication, we now
turn to the *problem* of communicating Christ to the contemporary world.

2
THE PROCESS OF COMMUNICATION

A number of years ago my wife and I were driving home from church, and our small son was sitting alone in the back seat, being unusually quiet. He apparently was thinking through his Sunday school lesson, for without any provocation he burst forth with the statement, "I don't like God."

Not knowing what to say, I simply asked, in what was probably an incredulous tone, "Why?"

"Because," he answered, "God killed Jesus."

A few years after that, we experienced a similar situation with our oldest daughter, who was then about eight. The incident occurred while she was a student in summer vacation Bible school.

"Mother," she said, "I know why Michael is so small." (Michael was a neighborhood boy who was unusually small for his age.)

"Why?" my wife asked.

"Because he doesn't have Jesus in his heart" was the matter of fact reply.

"Well, what does that have to do with size?" asked my wife.

"My teacher said that if you don't have Jesus in your heart you won't grow."

These two rather innocent stories (and their far-reaching implications) point to a problem Christian communicators must solve to be effective. In short, the problem is knowing how to build bridges between people. The failure to communicate Christian truth in both of the above illustrations was rooted in the failure to span the gap between the sender and the receiver. While the communicator may have had a good grasp of what he was saying, it was lost in the process of being filtered through the mind of the young receivers. Consequently, a communication of what was intended did not take place.

The *task* of the Christian to communicate Christ to the contemporary world cannot be adequately accomplished without giving serious and intelligent consideration to the building of communication bridges between the Christian communicator and his audience. In order to get this point across, I will discuss two issues: (1) the process of communication and (2) some theological considerations for building bridges between people.

COMMUNICATION AS A SCIENCE

An increasing amount of discussion has occurred within the past ten years over the problem of communication. With the recognition of communication as a *science*, the inquiry has become a formal, academic matter. Although there are differing opinions about what the science of communication is, it is sufficient for our purpose to look at the matter in general. For this reason I will set forth some generally accepted views on two matters: (1) what a communication model looks like, and (2) some factors that complicate the communication of the Christian message.

A Communication Model

In the most basic form of a Christian communication model, we recognize three components: the *message*, the *sender*, and the *receiver*. All three of these components are obviously necessary in the process of communication.[1] The process itself is not simple, however, for a number of variants must be taken into consideration.

First, there is the matter of the message itself. Although this aspect will be discussed in further detail later, it is important now to take note of the complexities. The major problem we have is that of understanding the Bible and its message within the cultural context in which it first appeared. This understanding is

[1]For a more detailed analysis of the process of communication, see James F. Engel, *Contemporary Christian Communications* (Nashville: Thomas Nelson, 1979), ch. 2.

dependent upon cultural, historical, linguistical, and theological inquiry. The problem is that the sender brings his own cultural, historical, linguistical, and theological presuppositions to bear on the interpretation of the source. The question is whether or not an accurate perception of the message by the sender has been made even before the communication between the sender and the receiver occurs.

This is the process called *encoding*. It is a complicated matter not only because it involves the possible misunderstanding of the idea that is to be translated but also because it involves the attitude of the sender toward the message. That is, the sender communicates both his subjective feelings toward the message and the data of the message.

Second, the problem moves in the other direction as well. Because the sender is communicating to a receiver, the receiver must filter the sender's interpretation of the message through his own grid. This is called the process of *decoding*. The one who hears the message brings his own set of cultural, historical, linguistical, and theological conceptions into the grid through which the messenger's message is being filtered.

A good example of this process may be drawn from Jeremiah 17:10. The King James translation of this verse from the original Hebrew reads, "I the Lord search the heart, I try the reins." A Westerner reads this and is puzzled by the meaning of the word "reins." Maybe he or she thinks of a horse's bridle or something like it.

But the linguist looks at the word in its original Hebrew meaning and discovers that the word means *kidney*. This is still confusing until the linguist discovers that the ancient Israelites regarded the kidney as the volitional aspect of man. It is here where the deepest thoughts occur, where man "makes up his mind" and determines the course of his life. Now that the linguist (or the sender) has understood this word in its own cultural, historical, and linguistical sense, he is in a better position to correctly encode the message.

Consequently the *New American Standard Bible* reads, "I, the LORD, search the heart. I test the mind." The use of the word *mind* is an excellent encoding for Westerners, who when they read (or decode) it, understand perfectly well what is meant. But if the same passage is to be translated for a culture that locates the process of thinking in the stomach, then the Western interpretation of the passage is inadequate. Consequently, we must see that the process of communication, the dynamic of encoding and decoding, is not static.

Good communicators always keep this process in mind. For Christian communicators, transcending cultural differences means we must know how to build bridges. But building communication bridges is not easy because of certain factors that complicate the communication of the Christian message, factors that I have already hinted at. Let me summarize them here for purposes of clarification.

As I already mentioned, *one of the major problems the Christian communicator has is understanding the cultural context out of which the Bible came.* Many well-meaning Christians have failed at this point. I do not mean to deny the principle of the perspicuity of Scripture. This principle advocates the view that the most essential message of Scripture, namely the gospel itself, is clear to all who can understand and needs no special superior mind or training to grasp. This principle recognizes the essential simplicity of the gospel and the power of the Holy Spirit to bring repentance and conversion. Beyond this, however, there is much more in the Scripture that *does* require intelligent and thoughtful understanding. Historical, linguistical, cultural, philosophical, sociological, and psychological tools, to mention a few, must not be set aside as irrelevant. If we are to communicate the message, we must know that message. An obscurantist approach to the Bible results in an inaccurate knowledge of the Scripture and therefore an inadequate communication of its message.

Another factor we must recognize is that the Christian message passes through the cultural context of the sender. It is only recently that we are becoming more aware of this problem. Unfortunately, many missionaries of the first half of the twentieth century labored under the naive notion that their own understanding of Scripture and the Christian message was equivalent to the whole truth. This error produced a static explanation of the gospel. The formulation of the gospel as well as the practice of Christianity was therefore entirely predictable. Even the customs, such as cultural taboos, worship forms, types of music, architecture, and Christian art, became uniform. Dedicated Christians failed to recognize that they had elevated a particular cultural form of Christianity to a position of truth. The cultural additions were made equal to the necessary transcultural ideas of the basic Christian faith. Communication of the Christian faith, then, became the transfer of a cultural understanding. This created numerous problems, particularly in the attempt to transfer the American cultural understanding of the Christian faith to a non-Western culture.

This conflict made Christians more aware of the third factor, namely that *the message must be communicated through the cultural context of the receiver*. Therefore, in the last decade or so we have seen the proliferation of theologies. We no longer speak of theology as a uniform discipline (although there are uniform beliefs that underlie theological thinking). Rather, we now recognize theology as human thinking about truth and perceive more clearly the human dimension of truth. We can speak of Black theology, Asian theology, South American theology, or African theology without being threatened. We recognize that behind all these theologies is a universally agreed content of theological thought that is articulated differently within various cultures.

These three principles, therefore, lead us to two other considerations. In the process of communication we ought to seek for *dynamic equivalence* or *adaptive orientation*.

Dynamic equivalence recognizes that truth does not always have to be communicated in a fixed form. It seeks to find, then, in the receiving culture a myth or legend or fact that corresponds with a biblical idea. This form then becomes the means through which the biblical idea is communicated. It is a point of contact, a bridge that crosses the span between differing cultures.[2]

An excellent example of dynamic equivalence is found in the correspondence between the Christian view of the incarnation and the Motilone myth that explains the similarity between the

---

[2]An excellent example is Don Richardson, *Peace Child* (Glendale, Calif.: Regal Books, 1974); and *Lords of the Earth* (Glendale, Calif.: Regal Books, 1977).

communal hut of the Motilone people and the home of the ant. Bruce Olson tells this story in *For This Cross I'll Kill You*. He was trying to tell the Motilone people of South America how God became man:

> Suddenly I remembered one of their legends about a man who had become an ant. He had been sitting on the trail after a hunt, and had noticed some ants trying to build a home. He'd wanted to help them make a good home, like the Motilone home, so he'd begun digging in the dirt. But because he was so big and so unknown, the ants had been afraid and had run away.
>
> Then, quite miraculously, he had become an ant. He thought like an ant, looked like an ant, and spoke the language of an ant. He lived with the ants and they came to trust him.
>
> He told them one day that he was not really an ant, but a Motilone, and that he had once tried to help them improve their home, but had scared them.
>
> The ants said their equivalent of, "No kidding? That was you?" And they laughed at him, because he didn't look like the huge and fearful thing that had moved the dirt before.
>
> But at that moment he was turned back into a Motilone, and began to move the dirt into the shape of a Motilone home. This time the ants recognized him and let him do his work, because they knew he wouldn't harm them. That was why, according to the story, the ants had hills that looked like Motilone homes.
>
> As the story flashed into my mind, for the first time I realized its lesson: If you are big and powerful, you have to become small and weak in order to work with other weak beings. It was a perfect parallel for what God had done in Jesus.
>
> But there were so many unknown factors in the way the Motilones reasoned. How could I be sure that I would convey the right thing?
>
> I couldn't. Yet I felt sure God had given me this time to speak. So I took the word for "becoming like an ant," and used it for incarnation.[3]

[3]Bruce Olson, *For This Cross I'll Kill You* (Carol Stream, Ill.: Creation House, 1973), p. 157.

A second way to bridge the gap between cultures is known as *adaptive orientation.*[4] This method allows the Christian message to become shaped to a certain extent by the culture it is entering. Of course, I do not mean that the substance of Christian truth is changed. Rather, the precise way of talking about truth draws from that which is known in the culture. This method avoids the error of making a person learn a Western culture before he can learn Christian truth. It recognizes that Christian truth can be understood within another culture without dependence on a Western mode of thought.

An excellent example of adaptive orientation may be drawn again from Bruce Olson's work. This time the example is from a conversation with Bobby, the first Motilone convert, as he was attempting to perceive faith and trust in Jesus. Bobby asked Bruce, "How can I walk on Jesus' trail?"

"Bobby," I said, "do you remember my first Festival of the Arrows, the first time I had seen all the Motilones gathered to sing their song?" The festival was the most important ceremony in the Motilone culture.

He nodded. The fire flared up momentarily and I could see his eyes, staring intently at me.

"Do you remember that I was afraid to climb in the high hammocks to sing, for fear that the rope would break? And I told you that I would sing only if I could have one foot in the hammock and one foot on the ground?"

"Yes, Bruchko."

"And what did you say to me?"

He laughed. "I told you you had to have both feet in the hammock. 'You have to be suspended,' I said."

"Yes," I said. "You have to be suspended. That is how it is when you follow Jesus, Bobby. No man can tell you how to walk His trail. Only Jesus can. But to find out you have to tie your hammock strings into Him, and be suspended in God."

---

[4]James Engel presents a good summary of both adaptive orientation and dynamic equivalence in Chapter 12 of *Contemporary Christian Communications.*

Bobby said nothing. The fire danced in his eyes. Then he stood up and walked off into the darkness.

The next day he came to me. "Bruchko," he said, "I want to tie my hammock strings into Jesus Christ."

From that day our friendship was enhanced by our love for Jesus. We talked constantly about Him, and Bobby asked me many questions. But he never asked the color of Jesus' hair, or whether He had blue eyes. To Bobby, the answers were obvious: Jesus had dark skin, and His eyes were black. He wore a G-string, and hunted with bows and arrows.

Jesus was a Motilone.[5]

These two examples illustrate that the process of communication is very demanding. If we would be bridge-builders between cultures, we must seek to understand clearly the message of Christianity in its own context, our interpretation of it in our own context, and the way it can be communicated into another context. The problem of building bridges suggests that the task of communicating Christ to the contemporary world is no simple matter. Nevertheless good communication is possible, particularly when we keep certain theological considerations in mind.

THEOLOGICAL CONSIDERATIONS

In building bridges between cultures we must charter our way between two dangers. On the one hand, there is the temptation to shorten the span between cultures by accommodating the Christian message too readily to another context. On the other hand, there is such a strong desire to retain the traditional understanding of the faith that some are afraid to take the risk of finding points of contact.[6] Consequently, the span between cultures is lengthened, and adequate bridges of communication are never built. To avoid these two extremes we must keep three theologi-

[5]Olson, *For This Cross.*
[6]A good discussion of this problem is found in *The Willowbank Report—Gospel and Culture*, Lausanne Occasional Papers #2 (Wheaton, Ill.: Lausanne Committee for World Evangelization, 1978).

cal principles in mind: (1) The content of the Christian message is transcultural; (2) this content is best interpreted within the cultural context of the Bible; (3) a faithful translation seeks to communicate both the content of Christian truth and the biblical interpretation.

A Transcultural Content

What is the content of Christian truth? By the word *content* I mean the essential, fundamental data of the written revelation. God has made Himself known to us by His works and activity. In the New Testament, God's major action is that of coming into the world in Jesus Christ, dying, and being raised. Around this event a number of other actions of God occurred.

We can trace the origins of this content by following the development of early Christian preaching in Acts through to the early summaries of faith in the second century. One of the earliest summaries of Christian truth is stated by Paul in 1 Corinthians 15. Writing to those who doubted the physical resurrection of Jesus Christ, Paul used as his argument for the resurrection of Christ the tradition of preaching that doctrine in the church. His claim was that *the preaching he delivered was the same that he had received*. The summary of this preaching was that "Christ died for our sins according to the Scriptures, and that He was buried, and that He rose again the third day according to the Scriptures" (1 Cor. 15:3,4). Paul implied that the basic content of the Christian faith had been handed down in the church and had been preserved in preaching.[7]

This same argument was used by Tertullian, Irenaeus, and other church fathers in the late second century against the false teaching of the Gnostics. At this time there arose in various parts of the Roman empire summaries of the Christian faith. The purpose of these summaries was to set forth the basic traditions of Christian preaching and faith over against the new and false doctrine of the Gnostics.

Scholarly research suggests that these summaries of doctrine,

[7]See Robert Webber, *Common Roots* (Grand Rapids: Zondervan, 1978), ch. 7.

which gradually became known as "rules of faith," grew up independently of each other in various centers of Christianity.
Nevertheless, the content of these statements was similar, and
like Paul, they all appealed to the fact that the truths contained in
the rule had always been held by the church everywhere. Here is
a good example of one of these summaries taken from Tertullian's
writings (A.D. 200):

> We believe one only God . . . , who has a Son, his Word, who
> proceeded from himself, by whom all things were made; he was
> sent by the Father into a virgin, and was born of her, man and God,
> Son of man and Son of God, named Jesus Christ; he suffered, died,
> was buried, according to the scriptures; was raised again by the
> Father; and taken back to heaven; and sits at the right hand; who
> will come to judge living and dead; who thereafter, according to his
> promises, has sent from the Father the Holy Spirit, the Paraclete,
> the sanctifier of the faith of those who believe in the Father, the
> Son and Holy Spirit.[8]

The point is that the basic content of Christian thought is
indispensable to the Christian faith and should be regarded as
transcultural. That is, the fundamental features of Christianity
cannot be dismissed as something belonging to the Semitic culture and therefore dispensable. These truths belong to all cultures. And if we are to communicate Christianity to another
person or another culture, we must communicate the doctrines of
the Christian faith that grew up in the New Testament church
and were recognized by the second-century church as essential to
the Christian faith. These include:

> The triune God
> The Creation (the event)
> The Fall
> Revelation
> Incarnation
> Redemption
> The Church
> The Consummation

[8]Adversus Praxean, 2, trans. Henry Bettenson, *The Early Christian Fathers* (New
York: Macmillan, 1961).

Once in a discussion between anthropologists and theologians, the question came up as to whether or not an adequate view of Christianity could be communicated without the Christian doctrines of creation and consummation. The point was made that some cultures are not linear enough in their thinking to care about the past or the future. My answer to this question is drawn from the early theologians of the church (and the history of Christian thought) who would insist that the doctrines of creation and consummation are essential to a Christian view of things.

If we are to communicate *Christianity*, then we should not communicate something less than the full content of the Christian faith. The image of Christ as the Second Adam or the Cosmic Figure cannot be understood apart from the doctrines of creation and consummation. The Christian message is that the whole creation has been reconciled in Christ and will be ultimately and finally restored in His second coming. If this is not communicated, then an inadequate and reductionistic form of Christianity has been passed on. A view of Christianity that omits creation and consummation can scarcely qualify as basic Christianity.

The Cultural Context of the Bible

In the previous section we extracted the content of biblical truth from the Bible and looked at it apart from its context. My concern now is to emphasize that an interpretation of Christian content has also been given within the Bible. If we want to communicate biblical Christianity, we ought to communicate the biblical interpretation of the doctrines we preach. That is to say that there is such a thing as a biblical understanding of God, creation, the fall, revelation, incarnation, redemption, the church, and the consummation. I recognize, however, that it is not as easy to agree on the interpretation of the content as it is to agree on what the content is. Here we rely on the work of the Holy Spirit in the tradition of the church and the work of Christian scholars.

An example may be drawn from an interpretation of the atonement. The classical biblical understanding of the significance of the death of Christ is put within the context of the cosmic battle between God and Satan. This battle is expressed in such opposite motifs as good and evil, life and death, light and darkness. John, for example, speaks of the light dispelling the darkness. But most important for our illustration is the contrast between life and death.

Paul clearly stated in Romans 5:12 that death is a consequence of sin: "Therefore as by one man sin entered into the world, and death by sin, and thus death spread to all men, because all sinned."

The picture is drawn throughout Scripture that death is more than a word describing physical death. It is a power of disintegration that permeates the whole created order, leading to its sure destruction. The New Testament image of Christ as the Second Adam and the Cosmic Figure is presented in terms of a conflict. Christ defeats the powers of evil. He destroys death so that it has no more power over man. Consequently man and creation are no longer under the dominion of death. They wait for the second coming with anticipation. At that event, the final act of Christ's drama over evil will be played. In the new heavens and the new earth there will be no more conflict.[9]

What we have here is the *best* explanation of interpretation of the atonement, but it is not the *only* one that has appeared in the thought of the church. The recognition that there are other interpretations of the death of Christ brings us to the third principle.

Faithfulness to Biblical Content and Interpretation

It is generally recognized that the translation of an idea from one culture to another must be made with reference to the origin of the idea. The best communicator of ideas always speaks in reference to the original source, to his experience of the idea, to his understanding of it, and to the culture through which it was expressed. Our real objective then, in translating the Christian faith from one culture to another, is, as Eugene Nida puts it, not "a change of content . . . , but rather a fitting of the same content into such culturally meaningful forms as will be fit vehicles for the communication of the message."[10]

[9]See Gustav Aulén, *Christus Victor*, trans. A.G. Hebert (New York: Macmillan, 1961).
[10]Eugene A. Nida, *Message in Mission* (New York: Harper & Brothers, 1960), p. 180.

However, because Christianity is transplanted from one culture to another and because cultures change, the translation of Christianity from one culture to another usually undergoes slight degrees of change or modification.

An example may be drawn from the history of the doctrine of the atonement. An aspect of the classical theory is that Christ's death is a substitution; that is, He died for me. But this is not a theory in the legal sense. However, as the doctrine of the atonement was filtered through the Roman legal grid, it gradually assumed the character of a legal enactment. In the early medieval period, Anselm developed it into a full-blown legal transaction between God and Christ for the sake of man. This view gradually became more important than the classical one and permeated the structure of Catholic meritorious theology as well as the justification theology of Protestantism. Only the East maintained its central emphasis on the conflict notion.

The point is that the basic framework of Christian truth (Christ died, was buried, and rose again for our salvation) was maintained. But the exact *emphasis* or interpretation given to that event in the Bible was not perfectly passed down. Instead, as it filtered through a Roman world-view, it was somewhat altered by the vehicle through which it was translated.

To a certain extent, all knowledge is altered through translation. To acknowledge this is certainly not a capitulation to relativism. Relativism is skepticism. The Christian faith, which stands on the clear teaching of Scripture, nevertheless recognizes the relative ways in which this truth is known.

A case in point is that of the Motilone Indians. The Christian message was communicated through their cultural grid and understood within the context of their frame of reference. To sense Jesus as a Motilone, as Bobby did, did not change the essential nature of Jesus. Later, Bruce Olson was able to more accurately present the Jewish, biblical Jesus to the Motilone Christians. This new knowledge in no way invalidated Bobby's original saving experience, but rather expanded his growing awareness of history and civilization in general.

Bobby's experience shows us that the saving power of Jesus can be adequately communicated without a reliance on the exact

biblical, cultural understanding of Jesus. Nevertheless, it is the
ongoing task of the church and of Christian communicators to
describe the biblical cultural context during the process of Christian education.

Now we must ask: What are the implications of these principles
for building bridges between cultures? What does this insight
have to do with communicating the gospel?

Implications

The first obvious implication of these principles is that we can
make a *distinction between the normative content of the Christian faith and interpretations*. It is clear that the normative
content of the theology of salvation is "Christ died, was buried,
was raised again." The biblical interpretation is also quite
clear—namely, the *Christus victor* notion. However, in the history of the church, other interpretations of the normative content
have been given. These interpretations, although not as desir-
able as the biblical ones, nevertheless have communicated the
saving reality of Christ. Many sincere Christian people who
demonstrate the fruit of Christ in their lives do so out of a
theology that has been shaped by a juridical world-view.

A second implication, however, is that *the biblical interpretation is preferable*. Certainly an understanding of Christ's success
over the powers of evil and death open up vistas for Christian
living and experience that are not perceived by those who have
only heard the legal view.

The third implication is that *the biblical interpretation is not
necessary for salvation*. God does not save us because we *understand* the classical view of the atonement. No, He saves us
because we trust in Christ, however imperfectly. God knows how
imperfectly His people understand Him and His ways. But He
also knows our hearts and knows whether or not we trust in Him
alone.

There is also a fourth implication that is necessary to remember: *The bridges we build are always imperfect*. Charles R.
Taber speaks eloquently to this problem:

There is in some circles a considerable reluctance to accept the full implication of the cultural conditioning of theology. It is sometimes objected that this approach undermines the basic integrity and truth of the enterprise, that it denigrates propositional theology and the like. But to relativize is not to destroy, it is only to spell out the fact that there are after all limits on what human beings can do, even on the basis of inspired scripture.[11]

There are several specific guidelines for building bridges between cultures that now become clear.

1. The bridge must be anchored in the full detail of the biblical framework. *We do not preach a creedless Christ.*

2. The bridge is most secure when it is anchored in the normative interpretation of the biblical framework. *We do not preach our own ideas about Christ.*

3. We must recognize the human element in all theological thinking. *Truth is always communicated through human channels.* Recognizing that "we see in a mirror dimly" makes us more reliant on the work of the Holy Spirit, which gives us the freedom to risk communicating.

In addition to these guidelines, there are some specific ways that recognition of various levels of understanding truth challenge our current method of communicating Christianity.

1. It brings into question the notion that we can communicate a partial Christ, i.e. a Christ who saves, but not a creator Christ or a Christ whose redemption is cosmic.

2. It challenges the assumption that our interpretation of Christian truth is normative, when in fact we often communicate an interpretation of the normative interpretation.

Finally a few remarks must be made with reference to the receiving culture. In building a bridge we are always concerned with making connections. In this respect there are several things we must keep in mind:

---

[11]Charles R. Tabor, "Is There More Than One Way To Do Theology?" *Gospel in Context* (Jan., 1978), pp. 4–5.

1. We cannot always expect to find a corresponding idea in the receiving culture for each aspect of Christianity. If this happens, there is no basis to assume that that aspect of the Christian faith is unnecessary. For example, we simply cannot ignore the Christian view of creation.

2. We must avoid building false communication through easy "accommodationism" or syncretism. Adoption of this method may result in the corruption of the Christian faith and the subsequent implantation of a false faith.

3. We must not shrink from a conflict of Christianity with world-views, false gods, and idols where there are few or no points of contact. The early church fought Gnosticism and paganism and made no concession to their false assumptions.

CONCLUSION

In this chapter we have examined the *problem* that is related to the *task* of communicating Christ to the contemporary world. We have defined that problem in terms of learning to build bridges between cultures.

We recognized first of all that communication must be understood as a process. This process involves understanding the message in its original context, admitting our own cultural framework through which our perception is filtered, and realizing that our communication must pass through the receiver's grid. For these reasons we must watch for points of contact with the receiving culture.

We then looked for theological principles that would enlighten our communication process. We concluded that the truth of Christianity can be known on several levels. We distinguished between such levels as the biblical framework (normative content), the biblical interpretation (normative interpretation), and our own interpretation of the biblical interpretation (cultural understanding).

This schema offers us some insight into the process of building a bridge from ourselves to another culture. It emphasizes the need to ground our bridge in biblical truth and cautions against communicating a partial faith or a mere interpretation of the faith. It furthermore keeps us from syncretism. Christianity must not suffer a reduction of its content or it ceases to be Christianity.

Having now stated the *task* of the Christian church as that of communicating Christ to the contemporary world and the *problem* as that of building bridges between cultures, we now turn to examine the *issue* of Christian communication.

3

THE AWAKENING
OF FAITH

Christian communicators desire to educate, to improve social conditions, to help discover natural and human resources, to reduce the mortality rate, and to improve medical and health facilities. These are all worthy issues, and they are also all related to the communication of the gospel. But the central and underlying issue that communicators must face is *the awakening of faith*.

Any brief survey of the history of missions from the Book of Acts to the present illustrates that the central concern of the church is to bring people to faith. Then, through faith, one's life in the world is reshaped. But how do we as communicators of Christ contribute to the awakening of faith?

In answering this question we have an opportunity to deal in a practical manner with the theoretical schema developed in the previous chapter. Often we seek to awaken faith through the level of a culturalized view of faith. In my opinion Western Christians often appear to *misunderstand faith*. Consequently, when we communicate faith we communicate our misunderstanding of faith. What we need to do then is to work through the outer culturalized perceptions of faith and again focus upon the biblical view of faith. This view will both reform our perception of faith and our communication of faith.

This chapter, then, will (1) set forth some culturalized misunderstandings of faith that we need to relinquish, and (2) set forth the biblical view of faith that we need to recover.

CULTURALIZED VIEWS OF FAITH

An essential feature of biblical religion is that it is a religion of the Word. The Word is that which is heard, acted upon, and obeyed. The phrase "Hear the Word of the Lord," which appears frequently in the prophetic literature of the Old Testament, is a statement that demands radical attention. The words that the prophets speak are not their own; they are the living, acting, powerful words of the Creator of heaven and earth, the sovereign Lord over all the affairs of man. The man who hears the Word of the Lord and decides to live in that Word is the one who "seeks the Lord." It is this Word that instructs Israel "to do justice, to love kindness,/And to walk humbly with your God" (Micah 6:8). His will is made known through His Word. Consequently, the failure of Israel is always related to their unwillingness to hear and to obey the Word of the Lord (see Amos 5:4–27).

This emphasis on hearing and obeying the Word is carried through into the New Testament, which is likewise a revelation, a word to be heard. The New Testament is an *announcement* demanding a response.[1] In this sense *hearing* becomes the technical term for the appropriation of the New Testament proclamation through which a person receives faith.[2] The person who *hears* the proclamation about Christ is the one who has faith. As Paul wrote: "So then faith comes by hearing, and hearing by the Word of God" (Rom. 10:17).

The only mark by which one is able to distinguish true hearing from purely physical hearing is faith. Faith is the active affirmation of what is heard. The one who hears but does not *hear* simply makes a mental note of what he has heard but never really does anything about it. He is "like a man observing his natural face in a mirror; for he observes himself, goes away, and immediately forgets what kind of man he was" (James 2:23,24). But the one who really *hears* is like the man who "looks into the perfect law of liberty and continues in it, and is not a forgetful hearer but a doer of the work, (and) this one will be blessed in what he does" (James 1:25). Hearing that is *real hearing results in obedience to what was heard*.

In the history of the church this emphasis on hearing the Word

---

[1]See κηρυξ and related words in Gerhard Kittle, ed., *Theological Dictionary of the New Testament*, vol. 3 (Grand Rapids: Eerdmans, 1965), p. 683ff.
[2]See πιστευω and related words in Kittle, ed., *Theological Dictionary*, vol. 6, p. 174ff.

frequently has been lost in the "systems of truth" or the methodologies men have adopted to clarify the truth. When the truth has not been allowed to "speak for itself," it has been inevitably forced into a foreign mold of thought. We turn now to three examples of categories of thought into which the truth-that-is-to-be-heard has been forced and subsequently perverted. They are the modern ideologies of *rationalism, romanticism,* and *existentialism.*

The Rationalists

The rationalistic approach to Christianity gives primacy to the mind. The mind is the tool by which the Christian revelation is proven. God's Word is not understood through hearing as much as it is understood through argumentation and proof. The emphasis of the rationalists therefore always falls on the credibility of the Christian religion. The motto "I believe in order to understand" is always rejected in favor of the prescription "I understand in order to believe." Faith is knowing what you believe and believing what you know. In this approach to Christianity there are no paradoxes, few mysteries, and almost no unanswered questions.[3]

The rationalistic approach to Christianity flowered among the second-century apologists, who were forced to demonstrate the credibility of Christianity as opposed to pagan philosophies. It also flourished among the great Schoolmen of the medieval period who took upon themselves the task of synthesizing the Christian faith with Aristotle's philosophy. More germane to the purpose of this work, however, is the modern form of rationalism that found expression among the seventeenth-century Protestant Scholastics and was later embodied in the rationalistic theology of the Enlightenment.

The rationalistic approach of Protestant scholasticism was anchored in a particular view of the Bible. In reaction to the Catholic dependence upon the authority of tradition, the Protestants of the sixteenth century shifted the focus of authority to the

---

[3]For a balanced approach to the relationship between faith and understanding see Arthur F. Holmes, *Faith Seeks Understanding* (Grand Rapids: Eerdmans, 1971).

Scripture as the living Word of God. Another shift occurred, however, between the sixteenth and seventeenth centuries. Scholastics of the seventeenth century lost the Reformation notion of the witness of the Spirit in the heart of the believer. They regarded this as a dangerous subjective doctrine of Scripture. Consequently they reduced the Bible to an objective textbook of truths. One could systematize the doctrines of the Bible and come by means of the mind to an understanding of the biblical message. The Scripture was no longer that Word which one *heard* and *lived by*. It had become the Word that was to be rationally understood and scrutinized.[4]

This objective way of viewing the Scripture, coupled with the elevation of the mind, set the stage for the Enlightenment's rationalism that shed the Scripture of its supernatural power.[5] The first step in this process was the conviction that the Scripture, like any other so-called system of truth, had to be subjected to the ordinary processes of rational demonstration. The second step was the common belief that man could determine universal religious principles apart from the Scripture. The final step was the reduction of the Bible to a mere human book full of superstition and contradiction. Man had elevated his reason above revelation. The Scripture, no longer the proclamation about life, was a record of primitive man's search for God, thus having little significance for modern man. The rationalist had "rationalized away" the Bible, and God and His Word had become superfluous for modern man.

One result of the rationalistic reduction of the Word of God is the disastrous overemphasis on fighting for the credibility of the Bible. I am not arguing against the proper use of apologetics or against the need to defend the Scripture against those who attack its inspiration and authority. The problem is that *the proper emphasis of the Word of God as the living and acting power of God has been neglected while the credibility of Scripture has been*

[4]An example of the analytic and systematic approach to theology among the Reformed theologians is found in John W. Beardslee III, ed., *Reformed Dogmatics* (New York: Oxford University Press, 1965).
[5]See Clyde L. Manschreck, *A History of Christianity*, vol. 2 (Englewood Cliffs, N.J.: Prentice-Hall, 1964), ch. 5.

avidly defended. For too many people the Bible has become an internally consistent, grammatically correct, and historically accurate document to be defended. Those who continue to overemphasize these points will soon replace the power of God's Word with the power of man's thought! The return to the Scripture as a true proclamation about life that is to be *heard* and *acted upon* is the only corrective. We must go beyond rationalistic apologetics!

The Romanticists

The romantic approach to Christianity gives primacy to the emotions. Proponents of this school of thought say *feelings* are the key to comprehending the Christian revelation. The emphasis of romantism therefore always falls on the subjective enthusiasm of the believer. Although the subjective approach to Christianity has expressed itself in a variety of forms, there are two contemporary views that are particularly pertinent. The first is a combination of the conservative school born out of seventeenth-century pietism and the revivalistic school born out of the eighteenth-century Great Awakening. The second is the more liberal school of thought introduced by nineteenth-century theologians (especially Friedrich Schleiermacher), which gave rise to twentieth-century modernism.[6]

It must be kept in mind that both the conservative and liberal schools of thought that emphasize the emotional aspect of man were born in the context of a highly rationalistic culture. In this sense the subjective emphasis is a reaction against the objectivity of rationalism. The pietists responded against the coldness of Protestant scholasticism; the revivals of Wesley and Whitefield awakened England from the slumber of Deism; the romantic response of the nineteenth century opposed the rationalistic spirit of the Enlightenment. In each case a corrective against rationalistic objectivity was being sought.

In an attempt to correct what was obviously the deification of the *mind*, the subjectivists tended to overplay the role of the *emotions*. Pietist William Law asserted that reason not only had no final power in religion but, on the contrary, was the source of

---

[6]Ibid., ch. 7.

all the disorders in man's heart. As a corrective to the misuse of reason, John Wesley emphasized the necessity of a personal spiritual conversion. Although the personal experience with God was nothing new (We can read of Paul's, Augustine's and Luther's, for example), the emphasis on *feeling* one's forgiveness was.[7] Wesley had sought for this *feeling of forgiveness* and according to his own testimony he received this feeling the day of his conversion. He "felt" his heart "strangely warmed." He "felt" that he did trust in Christ for his salvation.[8] No one would dispute the reality of this experience for Wesley, and no one should argue against his "feeling" forgiven. The problem is not his experience but the school of thought that has made this kind of feeling normative to conversion. To teach that everyone, in becoming a Christian, must have this kind of experience elevates the form and not the message and does not give proper recognition to the varieties of personalities and situations from which people hear the Word of God.

The major problem of the subjective school of thought is its *one-sidedness*. Like rationalism, it has chosen one aspect of man and deified it. The message of Scripture is thereby reduced to the narrowly conceived function of meeting man's emotional needs.

The Existentialists

The word *existential* needs some qualification. There are several schools of existential thought and much within these schools to commend. The emphasis on Christianity as a "personal" relationship that influences all of one's existence is good. These themes pick up on biblical concerns and act as a healthy corrective to overemphasis on reason and objectivity.

The existentialism I am concerned about is the school of thought that regards the historical character of Christian revelation as a matter of irrelevance and denies the proper place of reason in the Christian faith.[9]

Central to this school is the two-level theory of truth. On the

---

[7] See Bengt Hagglund, *History of Theology* (St. Louis: Concordia, 1968), ch. 31.
[8] This section of Wesley's journal is quoted in Manschreck, *A History*, p. 284ff.
[9] See Holmes, *Faith Seeks*, chs. 3 and 6.

one hand there is the truth of *Historie*, the truth of an event, a happening in history. On the other hand is the truth of *Geschichte* or interpretation of the event or happening in history. *Historie*, or the lower-level truth, is subject to historical criticism, but *Geschichte*, or upper-level truth, is beyond rational verification or criticism because it is interpretation. The existentialist classifies the Bible as upper-level truth, *Geschichte*. It is interpretation of history, not history.

Ultimately this two-level theory offers a supra-rational approach to truth. A man can tear the Scripture to shreds and deny its historical validity but still accept it as a truthful statement about life. For example, in this school of thought the truth that is in Jesus Christ is unrelated to His historicity. So while a person may conclude on the level of *Historie* (fact) that the historicity of Jesus is at best problematical and consequently irrelevant, he may nevertheless affirm the truthfulness of the Christ-idea on the level of *Geschichte* (interpretation). The genius of this approach is that a man can believe in his heart what his mind tells him is untrue. This leap into the supra-rational is faith—a belief in something that may greet the mind as nonsense. So man is urged to believe something *because* all reason is against it. It is absurd, and for that reason it is true. Grace may be described as the acceptance of our acceptance by God in spite of everything that may contradict it.

An encounter with the Christ-idea, however, verifies to some extent God's graciousness toward us. What one encounters becomes real to him; so both truth and reality are combined in the encounter. When one encounters grace through the Christ-idea, grace becomes real. Since the encounter is supra-rational, it lies beyond the field of rational inquiry and cannot be touched by scientific or philosophic argument. Such faith is safe; it cannot be questioned by the reality of this world; it lies above and beyond.

A basic problem with this approach to grace is that it leads to ultimate relativity. One can put anything one wants in that supra-rational upper-story. Someone may put Christ there, another Buddah, another Satan; but since no one's experience can be touched by rational inquiry, there really is no way to determine which, if any, is really true. Ultimately grace is the human feeling of being accepted and has nothing to do necessarily with the life, death, and resurrection of Jesus of Nazareth.

Critique

None of these schools of thought—rationalism, romanticism, or existentialism—are able to offer a truly biblical approach to apprehending the biblical world-view.

The rationalists have reduced the Word of God to a statement, alongside of all other statements about life, that must be verified in the same way any other world-view is verified. While we would not argue against the value of supporting arguments for Christianity, we would reject the rationalistic approach as one that reduces the apprehension of Christian truth to a methodology—this is a far cry from the Word that is to be heard and acted upon.

The subjectivistic school of thought reduces Christianity to the positive and warm feelings one has in the chamber of one's heart. The apprehension of Christianity no longer affects the whole person, but only a part. Christianity therefore runs alongside of life rather than being the central truth out of which life emerges. This highly personal approach to Christianity calls one to withdraw from life into the seclusion of one's closet. It does not hear the Word of God about *all* of life.

Finally, the existential approach to Christianity denies what it affirms. The very ground out of which a Christian view of life emerges is both accepted and rejected. The ground of the biblical world-view is deeply rooted in the concept of creation-fall-redemption. Supra-rationalists hold the idea as true, and yet reject the plausibility of these events as real historical truths. In the end the supra-rationalists' world-view carries with it no more certainty than that of the absurdists. He only hopes in hope without knowing what it is he is looking forward to in hope.

Notice that in each of the above cases the notion of faith has been filtered through a "system" or a "cultural grid." The point is, we are called to communicate *biblical* faith, not our interpretation of faith. So, let's now turn to an examination of the biblical concept of faith in hopes of "going through" the cultural grid and getting a grip on the biblical perception of faith.

A BIBLICAL VIEW OF FAITH

The starting point for knowing God is not conceptual thought nor experience but the "word" we live by. By *word* I mean that belief system by which we order our lives. The word we live by is the word we *really* hear and act upon. Further explanation is in order.

We meet life on the level of daily human experience. Life is our constant companion. The extent to which we are forced to deal with the meaning of life is determined by the particular situations in which we find ourselves. For example, encounters with pain, sorrow, and death confront us with our "limitations" in an unusually forcible way. In this kind of a situation, only an extraordinarily insensitive person will not think deeply about the meaning of life.

More common, however, are the less dramatic, somewhat humdrum activities of life that confront us every day. Our daily decision-making process is based on our underlying assumptions about life. Our decisions about behavior, thoughts, and opinions always relate to the word we live by.

Whether we know it or not, each of us is a product of our time. We are the way we are in part because of the people who have influenced us, the books we have read, the television shows we have seen, the places we have gone, and the things we think about. The twentieth century has contributed to the shaping of our lives—its sights and sounds, wars and crime, noise and pollution, and varieties of ideologies. What we have been, what we are, what we will be are all related to these forces that close in on us and demand our response. Each of these forces represents a *word*, a voice, that asks us to hear what it says and to act upon what we've heard!

The word we hear and live by is the word we worship. Think of all the words that demand our response.

The word of *humanism* proclaims, "Man is the measure of all things." It calls us to make man our god and to worship and serve the creature rather than the Creator. The word of *determinism* announces that man is nothing more than a cork on the ocean of life, tossed to and fro by the forces of life. The word of *materialism* tempts us to live as though matter alone is the true basis for life. We are to make the almighty dollar our goal, our highest value in life. The word of *relativism* announces that truth varies from man to man. Everyone makes his own rules and lives according to his own liking. The word of the *organization man* is to "climb the ladder," "be the person at the top." The word of *complacency* gives top priority to the establishment and to "security." The word of *despair* proclaims the ultimate meaninglessness of life, a journey from nothing to nothing. And there are more words—*technocrat, compartmentalization, neurotic, ad infinitum.*

These words, which represent an entire way of thinking of life, press in on us every day demanding us to hear and to live by them. *The word we live by is our god.*

Now let's look at hearing from another point of view. There is another Word that has entered into life, demanding our attention, our response. It is that Word of God embodied in Jesus Christ.

> In the beginning was the Word, and the Word was with God, and the Word was God (John 1:1).

> And the Word became flesh and dwelt among us, and we beheld His glory, the glory as of the only begotten of the Father, full of grace and truth (John 1:14).

The Center of the universe, the One from whom all things derive life and meaning, stepped into human history. He has proclaimed His presence. He has announced His lordship over *all* of life. He calls us to *hear* Him and to *live by His Word.* The person who hears the Word of the Lord Christ and lives according to it lives out of the context of a biblical world-view. Faith has been awakened.

True Hearing—Awareness and Obedience

The form in which hearing expresses itself in our consciousness is through *awareness* and *obedience*.[10]

Awareness is that quality of hearing that results in the inner

---

[10]I am attempting to provide a description of the process we undergo when Jesus Christ becomes the Word we worship.

sense of the presence of God. It is an ongoing encounter with the reality that God is there. Such awareness goes deeper than experience, although we are able to "feel" the experience to a certain degree. Rather, spiritual awareness lets us in on something higher and more powerful, something deeper and more sublime than words can convey or experiences can reveal. It expresses itself in a sense of wonder, amazement, awe, and renewed sensitivity to life.

When the Word of the Lord in Christ is truly heard, there is a response deep down in the inner man that says, "Yes, what I have heard is the truth about life. I am willing to risk my life that it is true. This is the Word by which I will allow my life to be shaped." Paul testified to this awareness: "And because you are sons, God has sent forth the Spirit of His Son into your hearts, crying out, '*Abba*, Father!' " (Gal. 4:6).

The awareness of God and our relation to Him and to His world result in the desire to *obey*. It is at this point where the concept of *the word we live by* becomes apparent. The Christian world-view is shaped in obedience to the Word. The Christian takes the Word seriously. He *worships* the living Word, Jesus Christ. That means he will do anything the Word commands him to do; he will construct his philosophy about life according to the Word. He will eat, sleep, and drink in the presence of the Word. In the struggle between the Word and words, he will consciously seek to say "yes" to *the* Word and "no" to all other words. He will live by the living Word that is brought to him through the pages of the written Word. His ultimate concern in life will be to serve the Word, the King, the Lord of life and man.

Hearing—Pre-analytical and Pre-theoretical

Now we must turn to the examination of an inference that has been made several times; namely, that hearing is pre-analytical and pre-theoretical. That is, hearing that results in faith comes not as a result of rational analysis or theory but by the Word of God. Thus, hearing as the means of faith stands in a special category of its own.

The Word of the Lord is addressed to the whole man; therefore, the man who truly hears responds to the proclamation of

Scripture as a total being, betting his whole life on its truth. Such a response confirms the biblical concept, that relates hearing to faith. Faith implies a willingness to live by that which has been heard.

Two biblical illustrations will point this out. In Romans 8 Paul wrote that the whole creation is waiting for the day of redemption. He wrote also of Christians who wait eagerly for the final resurrection. It was in this context that Paul wrote a beautiful description of the relationship between faith and hearing: "For we were saved in this hope, but hope that is seen is not hope; for why does one still hope for what he sees? But if we hope for what we do not see, then we eagerly wait for it with perseverance" (Rom. 8:24,25).

When a person *really* hears the gospel proclamation, he lives in the certain hope that what he has heard is true. He does not know everything about this hope, nor has he experienced its full reality; but this hope becomes certain by virtue of faith.

The writer of Hebrews demonstrated the same understanding of faith and hearing when he answered the question What is faith? "Now faith is the substance of things hoped for, the evidence of things not seen" (Heb. 11:1).

The author of Hebrews goes on in chapter 11 to illustrate this truth from the lives of the Old Testament saints who heard the Word of the Lord and lived by what they heard.

From a human standpoint, hearing always carries with it a gnawing doubt, for there is no way through reason or experience to prove conclusively the validity of what one hears. True hearing, then, is somewhat of a risk—one risks his life that what he has heard is true. From a divine standpoint, hearing is a gift given by God's Spirit. As Christians we do not "happen" to believe the gospel because of rational arguments or mountaintop experiences. Rather, ours is a conviction born by the Spirit of God that what we have heard about life is true. Faith has come to us as a result of the work of God's Spirit, not as the result of argumentation or experience.

The Rational and Experiential Content of Faith

Having clarified what is meant by the pre-analytical and

pre-theoretical nature of hearing the Word of God, we now turn to the examination of the rational and experiential content of faith.

The Christian faith does have rational content. The content of Scripture corresponds with reality and thus is rational. God's Word tells the truth about life. It tells the truth about God, the meaning of life, the significance of man, the human situation, and the re-creation of man and creation. Scripture "makes sense" because it is true to life.

Faith is not dependent upon proof. The point to keep in mind is that proof is a very limited tool when it comes to the ultimate religious questions of life. Proof never has and never will be the necessary means through which faith is gained. The most a good argument can do is bring support to the defense of the Christian proclamation (thus the limitation of Christian apologetics). Therefore, to say that the Christian proclamation contains rational content is *not* to say that the content is shown to be true through reason. No, the only way scriptural content becomes a personal way of thinking is through the work of the Holy Spirit. Through Him the proclamation of the Christian way of thinking becomes an *event*—a continuing event—a habit of life. But, it *is* a way of thinking, too. It is a definite point of view, a way of perceiving life. It is a reasonable way of thinking—that is, it makes sense.

Faith also involves experience. To understand this, we need to examine the meaning of the word *experience*. Generally we use the word *experience* in a particularized sense. We refer to this experience or that experience as a special event in life. It is in this sense that we speak of a "conversion experience." Although this is a legitimate use of the word, it tends to narrow the meaning of *experience* to unusual happenings.

There is a broader usage of the term *experience*. We can and we should refer to all of life as an experience. The word really has to do with existence. Existence itself is a continuing experience. We experience life from the moment we are conceived to the moment we die. In this sense we never escape experiencing existence. Now the Christian proclamation is experiential because it describes a way to live. It not only proclaims a way to think but also a way to live out what is thought. When we live according to scriptural truths, we are involved in a continual *experience of faith*.

To recognize that the true hearing of the Christian message is dependent upon neither reason nor experience is to chart a path between the two that results in the balanced affirmation of both. The scriptural proclamation we hear is reasonable because it announces the truthful way to think about life. But it is also experientially valid, for it proclaims the right way to live; and when we live that way there is a communication within us that affirms the rightness of our way of living. Faith therefore shapes the way we perceive reality as well as the way we live.

CONCLUSION

In this chapter I have defined the issue of Christian communication as that of awakening faith. The question "What is faith?" has given us the opportunity to examine both what we believe faith is (our interpretation) and what faith in the biblical sense really is.

The fact is that we tend to communicate our own culturalized view of Christianity. In the case of faith, Western Christians have filtered the notion through a cultural grid. Three more common grids are rationalism, romanticism, and existentialism. All of these are culturally conditioned philosophies that color our interpretations of faith.

Recognizing our propensity toward culturally conditioned faith, we are driven back into the Hebraic world-view and the notion of faith that was expressed in the context of the Bible. Here we find a correlation between faith and hearing. To hear something is to live by it. Thus, our calling as Christian communicators is not to get people merely to accept the content of faith, nor is it to evoke within them some warm and tender feelings about Christ. Rather, the point of Christian communication is to awaken faith in Jesus Christ as Lord and Savior.

Christian faith finds expression in terms of awareness and obedience. Awareness affects the mind. It creates a new orientation toward life. The believer perceives reality from the perspective of the incarnation, the redemption, and the re-creation of all things. His perception of reality is through Jesus Christ. Obedience affects the life. Life is now lived in obedience to the work of God in Christ. Thus the Christian has a new set of values, new goals, new purposes.

The issue of Christian communication is therefore related to all of life. Since Christ is Lord of the whole creation, the reorientation of man and creation through faith is the goal of Christian communication.[11] The question we must now ask is whether or not there is any basis for communication so broadly conceived.

---

[11]See Holmes, *All Truth Is God's Truth* (Grand Rapids: Eerdmans, 1978).

II.

A THEOLOGY
OF COMMUNICATION

4

THE BASIS
OF COMMUNICATION:
GOD AND CREATION

The Christian world-view does not begin with existence, or material reality, as though it were self-sufficient, autonomous, or all that is.

It is a fundamental axiom of Christian teaching that nothing in this world can be understood in and of itself. Christianity confesses a supernatural spiritual reality. Whatever man seeks to understand and know in this world must always be understood with reference to what stands beyond this world in the unseen dimension.

This axiom is as essential to the theology of communication as it is to the theology of man. Christianity presupposes that God is, that God has created, that God has revealed Himself, and that God in fact has come into this world in the Person of Jesus Christ.

It is my purpose in this chapter to show how the existence of God and belief that He has created the world sheds light on the issue of communication.

GOD: THE ULTIMATE BASIS FOR COMMUNICATION

The Scriptures clearly proclaim that there is only one God. The ancient Jewish creed affirmed: "Hear, O Israel! The LORD is our God, the LORD is one!" (Deut. 6:4). Paul reminded the Christians at Corinth, ". . . we know that an idol is nothing in the world, and that there is no other God but one" (1 Cor. 8:4).

But the New Testament clearly sets forth the teaching that Father, Son, and Holy Spirit are each to be called God. Paul wrote to the Corinthians, ". . . yet for us there is only *one God, the Father,* of whom are all things . . ." (1 Cor. 8:6, italics mine; see also John 20:17 and Eph. 4:6). Paul also referred to *Jesus as*

God in his letter to the Colossian Christians: ". . .in Him dwells all the fullness of the Godhead bodily" (Col. 2:9; see also John 5:18, John 10:30, Rom. 9:5, Phil. 2:6). And Jesus referred to *the Holy Spirit* as the One whom "I shall send to you from the Father . . ." (John 15:26). It is also striking to notice that the three Persons of the Godhead are brought together as one in the baptismal declaration (see Matt. 28:19) and the early Christian benedictions (see 2 Cor. 13:14).

The tradition of the church, beginning with the first century and continuing down throughout its history, has always affirmed the triadic nature of God. This is most clearly seen in worship practices in the church and in her creedal statements. For example, the earliest noncanonical statement on baptism stressed the necessity of being baptized in the name of the Father, the Son, and the Holy Spirit;[1] the earliest description of Christian worship recognized the Father, the Son, and the Holy Spirt;[2] and the earliest creedal statements affirmed the triune nature of God as well.[3]

Nevertheless, in the early church there were several heretical movements that attempted to explain the Godhead with an emphasis on singularity, dismissing the plurality of God's nature. The modalists argued that God was one but played three parts, appearing first as Father, then as Son, and later as Spirit. God, it was argued, was much like an actor who wears three masks—a single person playing three different roles.[4] Another group, the Dynamistic Monarchians, argued for an adoptionistic view of Jesus. To them, He was a typical man blessed with the presence of the Spirit. Because He did God's work, He was adopted into the Godhead as a reward.[5] Another faction, led by Arius, the most famous of those who rejected plurality in the Godhead, insisted that Jesus was simply the first created being and thus

---

[1]See Chapter 7 ("The Didache") in Cyril Richardson, ed., *Early Christian Fathers* (Philadelphia: Westminster Press, 1953), p. 174.
[2]See Justin Martyr, "Apology," *Early Christian Fathers*, ch. 67, p. 287.
[3]See Irenaeus, "Against Heresies," book 1, ch. 10 in Richardson, *Early Christian Fathers*, p. 360.
[4]See J.N.D. Kelly, *Early Christian Doctrine*, 2nd ed. (New York: Harper & Row, 1972), pp. 121-123.
[5]Ibid., pp. 115-119.

had the title "Son of God." But Jesus, Arius insisted, was not God for "there was a time when he was not."[6]

All these attempts to dismiss the plurality of the Godhead were rejected by the church in various councils—especially in the council of Nicaea (A.D. 325). But why? The primary answer to this question is that *the argument for the singularity of God did not correspond with the teaching of Scripture and the witness of tradition.*

By going back to the Scripture, it can be discovered that the argument for the plurality of the Godhead lies in those Scriptures that speak of the *intimate communication* that exists between the persons of the Godhead. First, the Scriptures speak of an I-thou relationship among the persons of the Godhead. The Father speaks of *"My* beloved Son, in whom *I* am well pleased" (Matt. 17:5, italics mine). The incarnate Son, Jesus Christ said, "I came forth from the Father and have come into the world. Again I leave the world and go to the Father" (John 16:28). And of the Holy Spirit, Jesus said, "When He, the Spirit of truth, has come, He will guide you into all truth; for He will not speak on His own authority, but whatever He hears He will speak; and He will tell you things to come" (John 16:13).

A second expression of communication within the Godhead is found in the love relationship to which the Scriptures witness. Jesus told His disciples that "the Father loves the Son and has given all things into His hand" (John 3:35). He also speaks of His love for the Father and tells how "I have kept my Father's commandments and abide in His love" (John 15:10). The Holy Spirit is also involved in this triangle of love for "He will glorify Me, for He will take of what is mine and declare it to you" (John 16:14).

James Orr, in his classic work entitled *The Christian View of God and the World,* explains what the love relationships within the triune Godhead mean in terms of perfect communication:

If therefore, God is love in Himself—in His own eternal and transcendent being—He must have in some way within Himself the

[6]Ibid., pp. 226-33.

perfect and eternal object of His love—which is just the scripture doctrine of the Son. This view of God is completed in the perfect communion the Divine Persons have with each other through the Holy Spirit—the bond and medium of their love.[7]

A third example of communication in the Godhead is found in the fact that the Son prays to the Father. In the garden Jesus prayed, "And now, O Father, glorify Me together with Yourself, with the glory which I had with You before the world was" (John 17:5). And speaking to His disciples Jesus said, "I will pray the Father, and He will give you another Helper, that He may abide with you forever" (John 14:16).

The biblical evidence forces me to conclude that *God is a God of relations and therefore a God who in His essence is characterized by communication.*

Implications

Obviously, the above statement has vast implications for human communication. Clearly, the ultimate in communication lies beyond the natural world. The ability to communicate is not something man invented. We are forced therefore to humble ourselves and recognize that the ability to communicate is from God.

Since communication within the Godhead is personal and relational, we may conclude that the same is true of all meaningful communication. The Father, the Son, and the Holy Spirit do not communicate with each other as if each were "outside" or alienated from the other. The Persons of the Trinity do not hold each other at arms' length. They are intimate with each other in a personal and relational manner; indeed, they share fully the common, divine nature.

The witness of triune communication is that it is always expressed through love. Love is the basis of good relations and, therefore, the context in which all communication should take place.

[7]James Orr, *The Christian View of God and the World, as Centering in the Incarnation,* 3rd ed., (Edinburgh: Andrew Elliot, 1897), p. 274.

Certainly "trinitarian communication" stands in judgment of our attempts to communicate in our impersonal and non-relational ways. It sets up a standard for communication and calls us back to the most important and basic ingredient of effective communication—personal and relational love.

CREATION: THE OBJECT OF GOD'S COMMUNICATION

The Christian doctrine of creation affirms that God created the world out of nothing, that God is not the world and the world is not God. At first glance this statement may appear to be doubletalk and have nothing to do with the subject of communication. However, a closer look will reveal the contrary.[8]

The doctrine of creation establishes a relationship between God the Creator and His creation. The Creator-creation relationship is certainly different from the relation between the Father and the Son. The Son is related to the Father by *generation*. He proceeds from the Father as God from God, light from light, fire from fire. In this sense the Son is of the same nature as the Father. Creation, however, resulted from an *act of God's will*. Because God willed the created order into existence it is *not* an extension of Himself but rather something that exists quite apart from Himself. The creation is, however, dependent upon the Creator for its continued existence.

Although God is free and independent of the created order and can act and create without it, the created order is significant in itself. Because it is not an extension of the essence of God and because it does not participate in the nature of God, it can be said that creation has its own essence. Yet, creation cannot be regarded as autonomous. Creation, to use a theologically familiar term, is *sustained* by God.

Now we can begin to see the connection between the God-sustained creation and communication. By recognizing the de-

---

[8]For a good treatment of creation and redemption see Emil Brunner, *The Christian Doctrine of Creation and Redemption*, trans. Olive Wyon (London: Lutterworth Press, 1952).

pendent nature of temporal and actual existence, we are able to see that *the Christian doctrine of creation affirms a relationship between God and His creation. God communicates with the creation and through the creation.*

Creation as an Image of the Triune God

In order to understand the relationship between God and creation, I will bring together the Christian view of God as triune with the Christian doctrine of creation. The early Fathers recognized that the divine communication within the Godhead was the archetype of God's work in creation. While the "inner working" of God is described in terms of the relationship that is sustained between Father, Son, and Holy Spirit, so the "outer working" of God reflects this three-fold inner working. Peter, for example, brought out the three-fold outworking of the triune God in salvation. He spoke of Christians as "elect according to the foreknowledge of God the Father, in sanctification by the Spirit, for obedience and sprinkling of the blood of Jesus Christ" (1 Pet. 1:2).

Analogies of the three-fold expression of God in the creation are found throughout the created order. St. Augustine's treatise *On the Trinity* is famous for drawing attention to these mirrors of triune reality. He grounded these analogies in the relationship of the creation to the triune God:

> For what does not bear some likeness to God, according to its own kind and its own measure, seeing that God has made all things exceeding good precisely because He Himself is the highest good? Insofar, therefore, as anything is, it is good, that is, to that extent it bears some resemblance though very remote, to the highest good . . . Certainly not everything in creatures, which is in some way or other similar to God, is also to be called His image, but that alone to which He Himself alone is superior, for an image is only then an expression of God in the full sense, when no other nature lies between it and God.[9]

[9]Saint Augustine, *The Trinity*, trans. Stephen McKenna, C.S.S.R., *The Fathers of the Church*, vol. 45, (Washington, D.C.: The Catholic University of America Press, 1963), book 2, ch. 5, pp. 328-29. See also pp. 277-78, 310-14, 322-28, 424-25, 462-63, 492-93.

This relationship between God and creation must not be described in either pantheistic or idealistic terms. Pantheism identifies the created order with God and thus implicitly denies the possibility of communication between God and creation. In pantheism the subject-object distinction is removed.

On the other hand, Platonic idealism fails to explain the relationship between God and creation because it posits the existence of eternal ideals other than God. This assumption limits the freedom of God to act creatively, denies creation as *ex nihilo*, and thus diminishes the reality of the visible creation by considering it only a shadow of eternal realities. Again, the true subject-object relationship is diminished.

The Christian view of creation affirms that no reality exists outside of God, that He created the world freely by His will, that the world is a reality in and of itself. For these reasons the images of God in the world are seen as expressions that communicate the nature of God. The shape they take in their "outer being" are therefore expressions of the relationship God sustains with His creation.

One such expression is creativity. The existence of the creation is an expression of the creativity that lies in the "inner being" of God. This means that all expressions of creativity are directly or indirectly "images of the creator."[10] For example, it may be said that creation has its own inner dynamic. When God created the world, He created something apart from Himself that is dynamic and has its own energy. Thus when God said, " 'Let the earth bring forth. . .' " (Gen. 1:24), He spoke of the energy and creativity that were *given* to the created order as an act of God's creation. Likewise, when Adam named the animals (Gen. 2:20), the ability to do so was an expression of God's creativity. God has communicated with the created order in such a way that His divine nature may be communicated in part by the works or the products of His creativity.

Another example may be drawn from the gift of love. We know

[10]For an expansion of this idea, see Dorothy Sayers, *Mind of the Maker* (London: Religious Book Club, 1942), especially ch. 3 ("Idea, Energy, Power").

by the testimony of the biblical writers that God is love. The love of God that we know chiefly through Jesus Christ, who demonstrated God's love by redeeming man, is of the essence of God. In Jesus Christ we have the "outer working" of God's "inner essence." Through the incarnation God has communicated with His world.

Illustrations similar to creativity and love could be multiplied many times. For example, the Holy Spirit proceeds from the essence of the Father. The fruit of the Spirit is "love, joy, peace, longsuffering, kindness, goodness, faithfulness, gentleness, self-control" (Gal. 5:22,23). Since these are the attributes of the Spirit, it can be said that whenever these attributes are experienced, communication has occurred between God and His creation.

The testimony of Paul is that all things are related to God. "For of Him and through Him and to Him are all things . . ." (Rom. 11:36). God is the origin of all things as Creator; He is at the center of all things through providence; He is the fulfillment of all things as the consummator. It is no wonder then that all things may be "images" of the Creator.

Satan—the Destroyer of God's Images

There is, however, one other Christian teaching that must be taken into account. The Scriptures speak of the fall. The church has always understood the fall in terms of a conscious and deliberate choice on the part of man to act independently of God. The fall described in Genesis 3 incurred a curse from God both against man and nature. Neither man nor nature sustain the same communion they had with God prior to the fall. The ground has been cursed because of man, and man has been sent forth from the Garden to till the ground.[11]

The biblical picture is that Satan as the "prince of this world" has established his reign of death in creation. Both man and nature are affected by Satan's presence. The presence of evil introduces into the creation a destructive and disintegrating

[11]This notion and its implications will be expanded in Chapter 7.

force. The very essence, or "inner workings," of Satan and his hosts stands in opposition to God. Their "outer workings" are displayed throughout the world. Nature has become the main instrument through which Satan communicates himself and his destructive desires. Creation is therefore in a defective state and thus fulfills its destiny quite inadequately. Consequently, the images of God in the world suffer distortion, even perversion, and are often hidden from the eye of man. Thus the communication of God through the creation is impaired.

However, the entrance of Christ into the created order is for the purpose of destroying the power and energy of the evil one and restoring the created order to its perfection. Christ Himself is the "image of the invisible God" (Col. 1:15; see also Heb. 1:3). He is the Second Adam, and as such He originates a new creation (see 1 Cor 5:17) that is to be expressed in the church and ultimately in the kingdom. The created order, which has been in "bondage of corruption" will be "delivered" and gain "the glorious liberty of the children of God" (see Rom. 8:18–25).

God Communicates With Creation

A major implication of the theology of creation-fall-redemption-consummation is that the goal of God for His created order is one of communion. Creation established a relationship between God and His world; the fall distorted it; redemption restored it; and the consummation will complete it. The communication found within the Godhead should be a matter of central importance to God's creation. That God desires to commune with His creation touches the very meaning of existence. God is a God who communicates with Himself and His creation. The hope of creation is that one day it will be in full communion with the Creator.

God Communicates Through Creation

The teaching that God is in communion with the creation gives us cause to recognize that *creation is a worthy vehicle through which God communicates*. The Christian doctrine of creation recognizes the significance of the created order and therefore rejects any Gnostic or Manichaean notion of the inherent evil in the physical world. God does not communicate to disembodied

spirits as though the physical were a barrier to communication.
No! God made the physical world. Therefore, in spite of sin, the
physical world is at His disposal; He may relate to it as He wishes.

That the existence and power of God is clearly communicated
through His creation is a fact supported by the biblical writers.
The psalmist declared,

> The heavens are telling of the glory of God;
> And their expanse is declaring the work of His hands.
> Day to day pours forth speech
> And night to night reveals knowledge.
> There is no speech, nor are there words;
> Their voice is not heard.
> Their (voice) has gone out through all the earth,
> And their utterances to the end of the world (Ps. 19:1–4).

Paul also declared that man can be aware of God through the
creation.

> What may be known of God is manifest in them, for God has shown
> it to them. For since the creation of the world His invisible attri-
> butes are clearly seen, being understood by the things that are
> made, even His eternal power and Godhead, so that they are
> without excuse (Rom. 1:19,20).

While God's relationship to the creation is known generally and
universally through the whole creation, He is known more specifically and particularly through *time*, *space*, and *history*.

In the first place, the biblical concept stresses the *revelatory*
nature of time and space. The heavenly luminaries are not simply
lights that "sit up in space." We can see from Psalm 19 that they
are *telling* the glory of God, *declaring* His handiwork, *pouring
forth* speech, and *revealing* knowledge. Their *voice* has gone out
through all the earth and their *utterances* to the end of the world.
The creation is alive, and the luminaries are in the business of
telling spatial time. The chief task of the luminaries is to separate
light and darkness, day and night.

The Hebrew people attached religious significance to day and
night. The light spoke of the Lord and darkness of the curse. We

see this distinction in Job's description of the continuing calamities in his life. "When I expected good, then evil came,/ When I waited for light, then darkness came" (Job 30:26). The prophet Isaiah referred to this idea in his appeal to Israel. He told them to pour themselves out for the hungry and satisfy the desire of the afflicted and then "your light will rise in darkness" (Isa. 58:10). It can also be seen in David's confession: "The LORD is my light and my salvation . . ." (Ps. 27:1).

The heavenly lights also speaks of God's goodness, love, and kindness. Psalm 136, which was part of the ancient Hebrew worship service, called on the people to "give thanks to the LORD, for He is good;/ For His lovingkindness is everlasting" (Ps. 136:1). Illustrations of His love and goodness are found in "the great lights" (Ps. 136:7), "the sun to rule by day" (136:8), and "the moon and stars to rule by night" (136:9).[12]

The above verses speak of the heavenly luminaries, the determiners of time, as means through which God communicates Himself. Another way in which God communicates through the creation is in *history*. History of course is part of time and space.

History, like time and space, is also revelational. There were times when God revealed Himself directly—through dreams and visions and by speaking audibly. But for the most part, God's method of revealing Himself was through history, at a particular time and in a special place. The exodus, for example, was an historical occurrence. God remembered the covenant He had made with Abraham, so He sent Moses, His human instrument, to His people and through him brought the Israelites out of Egypt. In this event God made Himself known. The people of Israel came to know God as one who faithfully kept His promises.

A good part of the religious life of Israel was introduced by this historical event. The celebration of the Passover, for example, re-creates the exodus event. In the celebration of the Passover, history is brought together with time and space as a means through which God still speaks. The exodus was an event of time, space, and history that continues to have meaning. The elaborate

[12]For an expansion of this notion see Thorleif Boman, *Hebrew Thought Compared With Greek*, trans. Jules L. Moreau (Philadelphia: Westminster Press, 1960), pp. 131-32.

physical preparation, including such things as the right foods, the ritual of remembrance, and proper dress, point to the universal timeliness of the event. God spoke to Israel in the original event. God speaks again in the re-creation of the event.

God Communicates to His Creation

In the New Testament revelation of God we meet a similar situation. God has made Himself known in a unique historical event—the incarnation. God the Son was born of the virgin Mary, lived among us, suffered and was buried, and on the third day was raised from the dead. In these historical events that took place in Palestine (space) in the first century (time), God is savingly known.

A central part of Christian worship is the remembrance of the birth, death, and resurrection of Jesus Christ. When the church gathers to celebrate the saving presence of God in Jesus Christ, she gathers at a particular time (Sunday, which holds special significance as the day of the resurrection) and at a particular place (wherever the Word is proclaimed and the sacraments observed) to re-create the historical event of the death and resurrection of Christ ("This do. . . in remembrance of Me"). God spoke in the first century. He still speaks to us in the remembrance. "For as often as you eat this bread and drink this cup, you *proclaim* the Lord's death till He comes" (1 Cor. 11:26, italics mine).

The exodus and the incarnation are the most obvious historical events through which God has spoken. It is important, however, that we do not view these as isolated events. Instead they ought to be seen as two uniquely revelatory events in a long chain between the creation and the eschaton. We are not dealing here with mere "snapshots" of history but with divine drama in our midst.

Creation was the event that initiated time, space, and history. In this sense creation should not be viewed as a "static occurrence" but as a dynamic beginning. Because creation has been disturbed by the fall, the ultimate goal of God for creation is its re-creation. After the fall God began to work within His creation for its re-creation. For this reason the communication of God in time, space, and history has an eschatalogical meaning. The Old

Testament points toward the coming of Jesus Christ. The birth, death, and resurrection are *fulfillments* of Old Testament expectations. But the New Testament events point to the consummation of all things; thus, the purpose of those events will be fulfilled in the new heavens and the new earth. In this sense, time, space, and history do not only reveal God's past actions but also God's future actions. Consequently, when we celebrate God's actions, He can still speak to those who are willing to hear.[13]

Implications

The major implication that God's relationship with creation has for Christian communication theory is this: *Since God regards His creation as a worthy vehicle through which He communicates Himself, man's communication of God's truth through the created order is forever affirmed.* This important communication principle will be developed and illustrated in the next chapter.

CONCLUSION

In this chapter I have attempted to set forth the reason *why* man is able to communicate. I do not believe we should study communication apart from this basic question. It is my contention that we need to understand the *why* before we can develop the *how*. In our pragmatic society we too quickly leap over the basic questions, which leads to gross misunderstanding of what we are doing.

There are two reasons for man's ability to communicate. The first is an ontological argument; that is, communication *is* because God *is*. Our confession of God is triune. He is, always has been, and always will be in relationship with Himself. God Himself establishes the principle of communication.

Second, God created a world with which He is in relationship. The world reflects the Creator (yet is not an extension of Him) and therefore communication is central. God's communication of Himself to the world is through nature as well as in time, space, and history. This establishes the principle that creation is a worthy vehicle through which God can be communicated.

[13]See Alexander Schmemann, *Introduction to Liturgical Theology* (New York: St. Vladimir Press, 1975), pp. 55-57.

5

MODELS OF COMMUNICATION: HISTORY, LANGUAGE, AND VISION

In the preceding chapter I argued for an understanding of communication grounded both in the triune God and in the relationship He sustains with His creation. In this chapter and the next I want to move into a more definitive explanation of the way in which God communicates with His creation and draw some specific implications for the task of communicating Christ today. We will deal, therefore, with God's special revelation of Himself, first through history, language, and visions and second through the crowning act of His communication—the incarnation.

GOD COMMUNICATES THROUGH HISTORY

At the heart of Christianity lies the message of redemption. The central concern of Scripture is to relate how man may be saved from the power of sin and enter into fullness of life. In this sense Christianity is not unique. All religions of the world are concerned with salvation of one kind or another. In the ancient world, for example, there were numerous redemption myths, each of which offered a plan of salvation.

So, what makes the Christian religion unique? One distinction is that the emphasis of Christianity is on *historical* redemption whereas the myths and many other religions of the world offer a way of *escape* from this world. At this point, biblical religion differs radically—it is religion of *this world* as well as of the next. For example, the Israelites were redeemed from Egypt so they could live as God's people *on earth*. The resurrection emphasizes the ultimate restoration of this world (see Rom. 8:18–25). The hope of Christianity, therefore, differs from the myths in that it has to do with man's life on this earth. This means that *in the here and now, in the events of life, in the very stuff that makes up day-to-day living, man may know and experience God.*[1]

God Communicates Himself

The teaching that God is known and experienced through history must be clarified.

To assume that historical events give us information *about* God is not enough. It is true we meet God in history. In history we learn of God's love, faithfulness, and mercy. But even more, through history God reveals *Himself*, not merely truths about Himself. His revelation is always personal and relational.

Another factor has to do with the nature of God's *actions*. For instance, through the gracious acts of the exodus and the incarnation, God communicated Himself savingly.

These insights obviously have implications for human communication; but before these are developed, we must turn to two characteristics of God's communication in history.

The first characteristic is that the events themselves always promise a further revelation of God. The exodus, for example, revealed God as the God of Israel and demonstrated the power of God on their behalf. It also offered the promise of a future for Israel. God did not simply act in a once-and-for-all fashion. His action on Israel's behalf was the beginning of a long process; He made a personal commitment, you might say, to see Israel through to the Promised Land—and beyond, for within the exodus was the hope for the redemption of the world through Jesus Christ. Likewise the incarnation, which was the fulfillment of Old Testament prophecy, also looked beyond this world to the death, resurrection, and perfection of the church and to the ultimate restoration of all things at the second coming of Christ.

A second characteristic of God's communication within history is that it is enigmatic. The apostle Paul is fond of speaking about

[1]For further development of this idea see John Baillie, *The Idea of Revelation in Recent Thought* (New York: Columbia University Press, 1956).

God's revelation as a mystery (see Eph. 3:3). For this reason he teaches that we see through a "mirror dimly" and "know in part" (see 1 Cor. 13:12). Theologians agree that God's revelation is never a full disclosure of Himself. He gives as much of Himself as the world is able to handle. It is progressive, coming slowly and gradually; then, in the fullness of time, a greater revelation of Himself was given in Jesus Christ. There is development to the revelation of God. His disclosure is as the acorn to the oak, the child to the man. Even now the fullness of His glory remains to be seen.

Implications

The implications for contemporary communication that can be drawn from God's historical revelation are many and varied. In the first place our communication ought to be *historical*; that is, it should speak to man's life in the world. It must relate to the everyday occurrences, the trials and troubles of existence. It must be a message to man in the *midst* of his suffering, oppression, poverty, hunger, and need. It dare not be out of touch with life.

Second, our message must have as its central concern the communication of God. It is not enough to give information *about* God or to merely relate God's past deeds. Instead, by the power of the Holy Spirit, it must be our concern to communicate God Himself.

Third, we need to recognize that we communicate God through *action*. We act in God's behalf. God is communicated through the action of His people. When we give a cup of cold water, express love, respond in kindness, relate in compassion, God is communicating His life in and through us.

Furthermore, our action ought not to be a once-for-all act but should hold out the promise of continuing communication. In this respect it is important not to communicate everything at once but to act and speak in such a way that God and His truth are expressed when the time is right for each person or group of persons to whom we are relating.

GOD COMMUNICATES THROUGH LANGUAGE

Language is a creation of God.[2] For this reason it is not at all unusual that God Himself should use language as a working vehicle through which to communicate Himself and His desires for the created order.

Language: A Worthy Vehicle for God

The Scriptures abound with references about God's direct and indirect use of language as a means of communication. He spoke to Adam in the Garden of Eden (Gen. 2:16) as well as after the fall (Gen. 3:18). He spoke to Cain (Gen. 4:6–15) and later to Noah (Gen. 9:1). In the history of Israel His direct communication through language became less frequent. He began to speak through prophets (Exod. 19:9) who spoke the word of the Lord to the people. Throughout the Old Testament and particularly in the prophetic books, refrains such as "thus saith the Lord" or "the word of the Lord came to me saying" appear repeatedly. A study of these passages show that the words of the Lord were understood. Man did in fact hear. He may not have obeyed, but that the word of the Lord was communicated, there can be no doubt.

God also used language to communicate in the New Testament. The angelic annunciations to Zacharias (Luke 1:12–23) and to the blessed virgin Mary (Luke 1:26–38) are prime examples of communication through language. Here the most important event in the history of mankind, the incarnation of our Savior Jesus Christ, was announced through the vehicle of language. The use of language in this event glorified language as a medium through which understandable communication may take place and put to question all doubts about the validity of communication through language.

Also, language is the medium through which the Good News

---

[2]I mean to suggest that the ultimate reference point for language is God. *He* made us linguistic beings. This does not deny, however, that language has not evolved and developed as man has intelligently employed this initial gift. See William P. Alston, *Philosophy of Language* (Englewood Cliffs, N.J.: Prentice Hall, 1964) and Arthur F. Holmes, "Language, Symbol, and Truth," *Imagination and the Spirit*, ed. Charles Hutter (Grand Rapids: Eerdmans, 1971), p. 3ff.

about Jesus was first spread. In Mark's Gospel we read the
original announcement of Jesus: " 'The time is fulfilled, and the
kingdom of God is at hand. Repent and believe in the gospel' "
(Mark 1:15).

Language was the key in spreading the gospel. At Pentecost
Peter stood up and spoke, "Let all the house of Israel know
assuredly that God has made this Jesus whom you crucified, both
Lord and Christ" (Acts 2:36). This is the message that was heard
in "other tongues." For God gave the apostles the languages of
those present in Jerusalem for the feast so that "they were
astonished, because everyone heard them speak in his own language" (Acts 2:6). The report of this occurrence leaves little
doubt that they heard and understood.

In the twentieth century the validity of language as a means of
communication has come under strong attack.[3] The assumption
that language is a product of man's evolution and not a gift of
God's creative act has removed the ultimate reference point for
the meaningfulness of language. From a Christian viewpoint,
language communicates because its origin lies in the triune God.
The creative act of God by which language was brought into being
is the final reference point for the validity of language as a means
of communicating. The fact that God used language in the history
of His self-disclosure affirms our use of language to communicate
God and His truth.

Language: A Worthy Vehicle for Man

Raymond Chapman addresses the question of the validity of
communication in an article entitled, "Language and Religious
Experience."[4] His major concern is knowing how we can discuss
God and the transcendent through things and actions that are
drawn from the material world. He suggests that the use of
language rests on two presuppositions. First, it must be recognized that "there is a reality which is the referent of the words we

---

[3]See Heinrich Ott, "Language and Understanding," *Union Seminary Quarterly Review*,
(Mar. 1966), pp. 275–93.
[4]Raymond Chapman, "Language and Religious Experience," *Church Quarterly Review*,
(July-Sept. 1961).

use about it."[5] Most of us have no trouble in making a connection between a word and its referent. For example, when we speak of car, house, wife, child, book, plant, or any number of familiar words, we can create mental images of what that word corresponds to in our own life. We also speak of intangibles such as fear, anger, pain, and grief; and we have some sense of what they mean because they are emotions we have experienced. Religious language is not exempt from this same process. It also must have a reference point, or it is meaningless nonsense.

The second presupposition on which the use of religious language rests is "that there is a correspondence between the transcendental and the imminent, a likeness from which valid analogies can be drawn."[6] This assertion takes us back to the theology of creation and the recognition that the created order expresses the triune God. Christianity does not affirm the platonic view that creation is a mere shadow of reality (the ideal). But Christianity does recognize that earthly things serve as "copies" and "shadows" of heavenly things (Heb. 8:5; 9:23; 10:1). These "copies" and "shadows" are very real in and of themselves, but they derive their ultimate meaning and significance from their originator—God.

Acceptance of these two propositions makes it possible to accept language as a means through which a real communication may take place. God has spoken through language. God still speaks through language.

The Use of Language Today

Nevertheless, Christian communication theorists recognize the difficulty of communication through language. Eugene Nida suggests that although "absolute communication is not possible, nevertheless, effective communication is always possible between people of different cultural backgrounds." There are, he believes, three arguments supporting this contention:

1. The process of human reasoning is essentially the same, irrespective of cultural diversity.

[5]Ibid., p. 323.
[6]Ibid., p. 324.

2. All people have a common range of human experience.
3. All people possess the capacity for at least some adjustment to the symbolic "grids" of others.[7]

If God is going to speak through our usage of language today, particularly when we are involved in cross-cultural communication, there are several principles we must keep in mind.

First, our *language must be appropriate to the context*. The problem we face is that of making appropriate translations of words from the biblical culture to the receiving culture. Much of biblical language is drawn from rural settings and makes references to things that other cultures may not have experience with in the same way. For example, the modern technological society has almost no contact with shepherds, sheep, vines, olive trees, and the like. The communicator must learn how to build bridges between worlds.

Second, *language must be related to personal experience*. It is one thing to speak of God as Father to a person who has had a good earthly father. It is quite another to use the term with the one who either has no father or a father who has been the opposite of what the term *good father* connotes.

Third, *religious language is only personally meaningful in terms of a religious experience*. It is essential, therefore, to bring a person to Christ as Lord and Savior before an extensive communication of the cosmic meaning and significance of Christ can be fully realized. One must believe in order to know.

The Problem of Preserving Essential Truths

One problem we face, however, in the communication of the Christian message is that of preserving the language of *essential* Christianity. Certain words convey Christian truth for which there are no equivalents. Such words and phrases as *trinity, deity of Christ, atonement, incarnation*, and *authority of Scripture* refer to truths that are indispensable to the faith. For the most part, these words introduce concepts that must be learned within the structure of biblical revelation. In this sense the com-

[7]Eugene Nida, *Message and Mission* (New York: Harper & Brothers, 1960), p. 90.

munication of the Christian message does involve the learning of a new language for many people.

On the other hand, there is a vocabulary that belongs to biblical Christianity but yet is not essential to the communication of the faith. Reference to Christ as the "Lamb of God" is on a different level than the "Son of God." An equivalent to Lamb may be found in many cultures, whereas the term *Son of God* is unique, transcultural, and must be taught. What Raymond Chapman calls "the poetry of faith" must be allowed in Christian communication. Christianity dare not lose its use of the imagination in communication. As Chapman says:

> It is here that the imagination can range freely, selecting from the complexity of human life those referents which may have symbolic power to communicate some aspect of Christian revelation. Here the only test for a symbolic mode of linguistic expression is its fitness to communicate, to arouse an appropriate response in the actual, present situation of a living individual. Here we may humbly follow our Lord in devising analogies, as He did in His parables, for the Truth that has been revealed to us. And just as society which neglects its poets and artists is in danger of a technically-obsessed decadence, so theology too must not lose its imagination.[8]

We may conclude that language is a valid means for communication for two reasons: (1) The origin of language lies in a creative act of God, and (2) its efficient use for communication is demonstrated by God's use of it in revelation. In our own use of words we must preserve the language of essential Christianity, making sure that what we communicate is biblical truth. Nevertheless, we are free to exercise our "sanctified" imaginations to create analogies and illustrations that communicate Christian truths.

GOD COMMUNICATES THROUGH VISION

There are numerous accounts in Scripture of God's revealing

[8]Chapman, "Language and Religious Experience," p. 330.

Himself through visual means. An interesting example is found in Numbers 12. Here God made a distinction between "mouth to mouth" communication and communication through "dreams and visions." (Direct communication seems to be a higher and more preferable form, at least in this instance.) Miriam and Aaron had spoken against Moses because of his marriage to a Cushite woman. Apparently they were calling into question Moses' leadership as a result of this marriage. God called Miriam and Aaron to appear before Him at the tent of meeting along with Moses. God met them in a pillar of cloud and said,

> Hear now my words:
> If there is a prophet among you,
> I the LORD shall make Myself known to him in a vision.
> I shall speak with him in a dream.
> Not so, with My servant Moses;
> He is faithful in all my household;
> *With him I speak mouth to mouth,*
> *Even openly, and not in dark sayings* . . . (Num. 12:6–8, italics mine).

Visions in Scripture

Although communication through dreams is sometimes looked upon negatively (see Deut. 13:1–6; 1 Sam. 28:6), dreams do appear to have a positive place in the biblical record. For example, God communicated to Jacob through his dream at Bethel (see Gen. 28:10–22), and Joseph was given the gift of interpreting dreams (see Gen. 41). More significant, however, is the prophecy of Joel:

> "And it will come about after this
> That I will pour out My Spirit on all mankind;
> And your sons and daughters will prophesy,
> Your old men will dream dreams,
> Your young men will see visions.
> "And even on the male and female servants
> I will pour out My Spirit in those days" (Joel 2:28; see also Acts 2:17,18).

While dreams have a place in God's communication to man, the use of visions appears to have more force and significance. The visionary material of Scripture has gained wide usage in the church and has resulted in the development of liturgy, music, and art as continuing forms of communication. Think, for example, of the images present in the vision of Isaiah, who saw the Lord

> . . . sitting on a throne, lofty and exalted, with the train of His robe filling the temple. Seraphim stood above him each having six wings; with two he covered his face, and with two he covered his feet, and with two he flew. And one called to the other and said: Holy, Holy, Holy is the LORD of hosts, the whole earth is full of His glory (Isa. 6:1–3).

This vision, along with a similar one of John's in Revelation 4 and 5, has continued to inspire Christians throughout the centuries. The vision of heavenly worship became a basis for the development of worship within the early church. The beauty and pageantry of Byzantine worship, for example, is patterned after the glory and majesty surrounding Christ on His throne. The refrain "Holy, Holy, Holy" is central to Roman Catholic, Eastern Orthodox, and Anglican worship and has inspired a major hymn in Protestant worship. The centrality of the throne has inspired works of art and architecture.

Other visions that have had a similar effect on the church include Ezekiel's (see chapters 1–3, 8–11), Jeremiah's (see chapter 13), Daniel's (see 1:17, 2:19, and chapters 7–10), Amos's (see chapters 7–9), and John's (see the Book of Revelation). In these visions, pictures, portraits, and demonstrations, God speaks to man through his senses.

Man is not merely a thinking creature, as we have made him in the West, but a creature of senses as well. Eugene Peterson captures the importance of sense communication in these words:

> Auditory and visual materials are most apparent in the Apocalypse. Tactile, olfactory, gustatory senses are peripherally represented. Hearing is basic. Underneath the message to be heard is the experience of hearing: "He who has ears let him hear!" Hear what? Never mind *what*, let him *hear*. Resonance is set up. Communication is established. God's voice and man's ears are united.

Hearing is joined with seeing. The two senses operate in tandem. The testimony in the first chapter, "I turned to see the voice . . . ," sets the tone. Ears and eyes are put to interacting and complementary use. Sounds of voices, thunders and songs, fill the air. Silence is significant. Sights of colorful, composite beats, a magnificent statuary Christ, visually composite women, and precious gems are rich fare for the eyes. A documentation of the sensory material of ear and eye would repeat nearly every line of the book. . . .

Its impact through the centuries has been basically sensory rather than mental. Men have not gotten new ideas out of the Apocalypse—they have found new feelings.[9]

We must now ask an important question that faces all Christian communicators: What implications for contemporary communication can be made from God's use of visual communication? To answer this question, there are several principles that must be set forth.

Principles for Visual Communication

To begin with, modern social psychology teaches us that groups find their meaning, identity, and connections with the past through images, pictures, and ceremonies that have been passed down and preserved for them through the centuries. Persons maintain their consciousness more through ritual than through language or logic. This is particularly obvious in the Third World and in the minority ethnic groups in America. The Scandanavian, Polish, Hungarian, and Ukrainian festivals, customs, special days, and ceremonies have a significance far beyond a verbal description of them. The acting out of these ceremonies preserves the memory and communicates an identity.

Indeed, ritual lies at the very heart of biblical memory. The Passover is an excellent example of the ceremonial re-creation of a significant event. The memory of Israel centers on God's action in history when He brought them up out of the land of Egypt. Every year for centuries devout Jews have reproduced Exodus

[9]Eugene H. Peterson, "Apocalypse: The Medium Is the Message," *Theology Today* (July, 1969), pp. 137–38.

12 in the most minute detail as a commemoration of the event that gave shape to their history and continues to give meaning to their present lives.

This is also true with the Christian church. Jesus transformed the ritual of the Passover into an event that is now celebrated in *remembrance* of His death and resurrection. We are a Eucharistic community, and the celebration of the Lord's Supper communicates our continuity with the past and our belongingness to all others throughout history and around the world who join in celebration of the Christ-event.

Second, *the stimulation of the imagination through visual images reaches man in the emotive aspect of his being.* In a world that is modeled after science, as is the Western world, truth is confined to factual correspondence. In this frame of reference there is seldom any place for the communication of truth through the imagination. Metaphor, symbol, poetry, and the apocalyptic become superfluous. The biblical use of the visual, however, speaks against such a limited view of communication and affirms the place of the visual.[10]

I recently witnessed a demonstration of the visual in an ordination service. In the charge to the ordained, the speaker communicated by word and sight. After calling the soon-to-be-ordained man to stand with him in the pulpit, he commenced speaking to him directly, centering his words around the major symbols of ministry.

Handing him a *cross*, he spoke of the central place of Christ in his ministry.

Handing him a *Bible*, he reminded him of the significance of the Word as the major tool of his ministry.

Handing him a *chalice*, he recalled the worship of the church and the minister's responsibility to gather his people around the Lord's Table.

Handing him a *book of prayer*, he commented on his calling to be a man of prayer for his people.

[10]See Edward N. McNulty, *Gadgets, Gimmicks and Grace* (St. Meinard, Ind.: Abbey Press, 1976).

In this case the visual symbols of ministry made a powerful impact both on the one to be ordained and on the congregration because they spoke to the imagination and communicated more than words alone.

A third matter to keep in mind is that the use of *the visual ought not to be out of contact with the receiver's social and cultural reality*. The point is, we should not create a visionary form of communication just to have visual images. Visual images must be rooted in truth and expressed in symbols that have correspondence with the receiver's experience. In the New Testament the images of Messiah, Lord, people, body, New Jerusalem, Babylon, salt, light, and vine were immediately relevant because they were within the experience of the one who heard.[11]

For example, Bruce Olson tells the story of God's banana stalk. It was a common belief among the Motilone Indians that God would some day come to them through the banana stalk. One day, in a conversation with several Indians about this legend, an Indian split open a banana stalk for purposes of illustration. When Bruce saw the inner leaves falling out like pages from the Bible, he immediately reached for his Bible and proclaimed "here is God's banana stalk." He flipped the pages as the Indians stared in wonderment. Bruce declared to them that this banana stalk (the Bible) contained the words of God. Here was a symbol that corresponded with their experience, one that made sense and communicated God's truth to them without in any way demeaning the significance of God's Word.[12]

Implications

As our age is becoming more and more dependent on the visual through television and other visual media, we need to become more aware of the use of the visual as a means of communicating God's truth.

It is important to note that *God does not limit Himself to words*

---

[11]For further development of these ideas, see Amos N. Wilder, "Social Symbol and the Communication of the Gospel," *Christianity and Crisis*, (Dec. 12 1960).
[12]Bruce Olson, *For This Cross I'll Kill You* (Carol Stream, Ill.: Creation House, 1973), p. 156.

as the only means of communication. In the Western world, and particularly in Protestant evangelicalism, we have become addicted to the rational, the discursive, and the dogmatic. Much of our world is now realizing the poverty of this one-sided approach to reality. The rise of the occult, the cults, and the emphasis on Eastern thought are all expressions of our desire for the "beyond" in the midst of life. If we are to communicate the gospel of Christ effectively we must go beyond our enslavement to words and tap the explosive power of the imaginative. Perhaps we will once again recapture the mystery of the cross and the experience of glory that lies at the heart of the Christian faith.

A major implication of God's use of the visionary as a means of communicating Himself is that we *ought to examine more closely ways of communicating the gospel through visual means.* Amos Wilder has spoken to this issue in these words:

> Old words do not reach across the new gulfs, and it is only in vision and oracle that we can chart the unknown and new-name creatures . . . the structures of faith and confession have always rested in hierophanies and images. But in each new age and climate the theopoetic of the church is reshaped in inseparable relation to the general imagination of the time.[13]

CONCLUSION

In this chapter I have attempted to explore God's method of communication with man. It is clear from our exploration of God's use of *history, language,* and *vision* that these modes of communication are sanctioned by God.

A theology of communication dare not disregard the significance of these models either by ignoring or demeaning any one of them. God has ordained them all as worthy vehicles for communication. A rejection of one or the other through choice or neglect results in a limitation of the means available for the communication of the gospel.

We must not stand in the way of communicating God's truth!

---

[13]Amos N. Wilder, "Theology and Theopoctic," *Christian Century* (May 23, 1973), p. 593.

6
MODELS
OF COMMUNICATION:
THE INCARNATION

Even though God has made Himself known to us through history, language, and vision, the climax of His self-communication is in the incarnation. Here, in this great act of humility, He became one of us and communicated with us face to face.

The writer of Hebrews extols the incarnation this way: "God . . . has in these last days *spoken* to us by His Son . . ." (Heb. 1:1,2). Matthew declares that Christ's birth means "God with us" (Matt. 1:23). John understands the incarnation as the "Word became flesh" (John 1:14).

Whatever words one may use to describe the incarnation, it is an important fact that all Christians, whether labeled Roman Catholic, Eastern Orthodox, Protestant, Pentecostal, or Evangelical, recognize the *centrality* of the incarnation to God's communication with man. Here we are on common ground with all Christians.

INCARNATIONAL COMMUNICATION

The incarnation is the focal point of God's communication with man. That is, all forms of communication used by God are expressed in His personal communication with man through Jesus Christ.

For example, the New Testament emphasizes the *historical* character of the incarnation. It draws a line backward from Christ to creation and forward from Christ to the consummation.[1] In this way the New Testament brings together creation-

[1] For a full treatment of this idea see Oscar Cullman, *Christ and Time* (London: SCM Press, 1951).

redemption-consummation in a single line with Christ at the center. The accent is on the cosmic significance of Christ, in whom and through whom all things are perceived and find their meaning.

Next, the ultimate revelation of God took place in time and space. The fact that time has been recorded in ever-*decreasing* numbers before Christ's birth and in ever-*increasing* numbers after His birth emphasizes the time character of the incarnation. The facts about where Christ was born (Bethlehem of Judea; see Matt. 2:4,5), where He grew up (Nazareth; see Matt. 2:23), where He taught (Galilee; see Matt. 3:13), and where He died (Jerusalem; see Luke 13:33) demonstrate the spatial location of Christ.

Furthermore, the elements of *language* and *vision* are found in the incarnation. The care taken to preserve the words and teachings of Jesus (e.g. in Matt. 5–7) shows the use of language in communication. Finally, the recognition that God was present in the here and now through Jesus (John 1:1,2,4,14,18) stresses the visual character of His presence. He is, as the apostle Paul stated, "the image of the invisible God" (Col. 1:15). *The incarnation, then, is not only the crowning event of God's communication with man but also that event in which all other forms of God's communication with man are embodied.*

Implications

Given the importance of the incarnation as a means through which God communicated Himself to man, we must ask, then, about the implications of the incarnation for communication today.

We may begin by comparing the significance of the incarnation with that of the Trinity. The Trinity, as argued in the previous chapter, is the ontological ground for communication. It is the basis for communication that stands "outside" of the created order. It is eternal and not dependent on time, space, or history.

The incarnation, on the other hand, is the "earthly" foundation of communication. Although the thought of the incarnation existed in the mind of God and was agreed upon in the Trinity, the actualization of the thought was dependent on time, space, and history. In this sense the incarnation may be referred to as the *earthly ground of communication*. John Warwick Montgomery expresses it this way: "The word entered our historical framework in the most literal sense, and thus specifically hallowed the use of communication in imparting divine Truth."[2]

The Model of Communication

Jesus is also *the* model of communication. His way of communicating stands as the ultimate earthly reference point for a Christian theory of communication.

Before looking at Jesus' communication methods, let's examine principles for good communication held by two experts.

Wilbur Schramm has set forth four "proper conditions for communication."

1. The message must be so designed and delivered as to gain the attention of the intended receiver.
2. The message must employ signs that refer to experience common to both sender and receiver, so as to "get the meaning across."
3. The message must arouse personality needs in the receiver and suggest some ways to meet those needs.
4. The message must suggest a way to meet those needs that is appropriate to the group situation in which the receiver finds himself at the time when he is moved to make the desired response.[3]

These four conditions are almost parallel to the four principles of communication theory that Charles Kraft draws from Jesus' approach to communication. In an article entitled "The Incarnation, Cross-cultural Communication, and Communication Theory," Kraft cites the following four principles:

[2]John Warwick Montgomery, "Mass Communication and Scriptural Proclamation," *The Evangelical Quarterly*, (Jan.–March 1977), p. 11.
[3]Wilbur Schramm, "Procedures and Effects of Mass Communication," *Mass Media and Education: The 53rd Yearbook of the National Society for the Study of Education, Part 2*, ed. Nelson B. Henry (Chicago: University of Chicago Press, 1954), p. 121. Quoted by Montgomery, "Mass Communication," p. 12.

1. For information to be conveyed accurately, both the giver and the receiver of the information must operate within the same frame of reference.
2. Within a frame of reference, the greater the predictability . . . of the message, the smaller the impact of that message and, conversely, the lower the predictability the greater the impact of the message.
3. The greater the specificity of the form in which the material is presented, the greater the impact.
4. Something discovered by the receptor of the messages has greater impact than something presented in pre-digested, generalized form by the communicator.[4]

A brief glance at these two sets of principles brings to mind several corresponding examples from the life of Jesus.

PRINCIPLES FOR INCARNATIONAL COMMUNICATION

The Attention-getting Element

The incarnation contains attention-getting elements. The annunciation passages suggest that God first spoke to those persons who were longing and waiting for the coming of Christ. Elizabeth, Mary, Simeon, and others were singled out to receive the glad tidings.

Gradually, however, the attention of more people began to be fixed on Jesus through the unusual occurrences in His life. Events such as Christ's display of wisdom in the temple at the age of twelve, His baptism, and the events at the beginning of His ministry (such as turning water into wine) stirred the crowd's interest.

Although Jesus never involved Himself in the bizarre (as Jeremiah did), He nevertheless was a controversial Person who was never afraid to do the unusual. A brief reading of any one of

[4]Charles K. Kraft, "The Incarnation, Cross-Cultural Communication, and Communication Theory," *Evangelical Missions Quarterly* (Fall, 1973), pp. 278–82.

the Gospels quickly affirms this assertion. He spoke to a Samaritan woman, picked grain on the Sabbath, stilled the storm, befriended tax collectors and harlots, ate with sinners, castigated the wealthy, insulted the Pharisees, threw the money-changers from the temple, and raised the dead.

Obviously, contemporary communicators cannot and should not try to duplicate all of these actions. However, the principle is a good one. If we are to communicate the Christian message, the attention of the receiver is a necessary prerequisite to effective communication. This is not to suggest that Jesus did these things to get attention. Rather, His message was so counter-cultural (in the sense that it had to do with God's kingdom) that the very presentation of the kingdom and its claims were set against the status quo. Christian communicators need to remember that when the Christian message is set forth in such a way that it is *no different* from the prevailing culture (or the other individual's lifestyle, in the case of personal witness), the communication fails to create a context in which the message being communicated stands out in bold relief. Christ came to set forth the kingdom and its demands. His description of the kingdom created an image so different from the sin-permeated culture that it automatically gained the hearer's attention. It put the receiver in a position where he had to make a choice, the alternatives were clear.

If what we are presenting is not essentially different from that which the receiver already has, there is no point in attempting to communicate. *Thus, the attention-getting element in Christian communication has primarily to do with the content of kingdom-preaching and not mere gimmicks.*

Identifying With the Human Situation

The incarnation also contains the element of identification. That God became a member of the human race is attested to in the New Testament and the early creeds. For this reason, the humanity of Jesus is an essential teaching of the Christian faith.

In the New Testament period questions were raised about the authentic humanity of Jesus. The way these questions were answered emphasizes the crucial nature of confessing Jesus as human. John insisted, ". . . Every spirit that confesses that Jesus

Christ has come in the flesh is of God, and every spirit that does not confess that Jesus Christ has come in the flesh is not of God" (1 John 4:2,3). When Paul wrote to the Corinthians who doubted the physical resurrection of Jesus, he insisted, "And if Christ is not risen, then our preaching is vain and your faith is also vain" (1 Cor. 15:14). The battle with those who denied the humanity of Jesus continued into the second century. But the orthodox doctrine that emphasizes the actual tangible reality of the presence of God in the world has prevailed.

Jesus identified not only with humanity but also with the *social context* of the first century. A brief survey of the Gospels makes this point abundantly clear. He was born "in the days of Herod, the king of Judea" (Luke 1:5). Although the references to His childhood are scanty, there is enough evidence to suggest a typical social context. He belonged to a family, learned a trade, and traveled with His parents. He spoke the language of the people, attended synagogue school, and learned the Old Testament and the traditions of His people. During His ministry He traveled in Palestine, made friends with people, ate the local food, and lived a life that was not externally different from many others of His social class.

Jesus' identification with us bears a significant implication for communication. It is this: *The incarnation is the perfect model of communication.*

In his letter to the Philippians Paul points to this fact. Apparently there was a squabble going on between two women in the Philippian church and their followers (see Phil. 4:2). Paul may have had this division in mind as he addressed the Philippian people.

In the opening sentences of Paul's letter, the word *all* appears several times as though to show his impartiality regarding any divisions in the church. His remembrance of them in prayer was "for you all." He was sure that God who began a good work in them would bring it to completion. "It is right for me to think this of you *all*, because I have you in my heart . . . you *all* are partakers with me of grace," and furthermore, "God is my witness, how greatly I long for you all with the affection of Jesus Christ" (see Phil. 1:3–11, italics mine).

At the end of the first chapter Paul became more specific. He urged them to "let your conduct be worthy of the gospel of Christ" and hoped to see them "stand fast in *one* spirit, with *one* mind striving *together* for the faith of the gospel" (Phil. 1:27, italics mine).

In the beginning of chapter two Paul dealt directly with the problem of schism. He asked the believers to be "like minded, having the same love, being of one accord, of one mind" (Phil. 2:2). They were not to do anything from "selfish ambition or conceit, but in lowliness of mind let each esteem another better than himself" (Phil. 2:3). They were not only to look out for their own interests "but also for the interests of others" (Phil. 2:4).

Finally, the climax of his argument was made by citing the Incarnation.

> Let this mind be in you which was also in Christ Jesus, who, being in the form of God, did not consider equality with God something to be grasped, but emptied Himself by taking the form of a servant, and coming in the likeness of men. And being found in appearance as a man, He humbled Himself and became obedient to the point of death, even the death of the cross" (Phil. 2:5–8).

The doctrine of the incarnation was no abstract idea for Paul. It had specific implications for living. Here, for the Philippian church, we see how it applied to the problem of communication. If Euodia and Syntyche and their followers were to communicate and restore a broken relationship, they had to break down the walls that separated them from each other, and having the mind of Christ within them they needed to "put themselves in the other person's shoes."

The incarnation, therefore, is the ultimate reference point for all identification. In the incarnation God set forth the standard for communication. If we would reach others as God reached us, we must be willing to identify with the very life, the social context, and the needs of those to whom we wish to communicate. [5]

[5]This point is also made by Charles Kraft and expanded in "God's Model for Cross-Cultural Communication—the Incarnation," *Evangelical Missions Quarterly* (Summer, 1973), pp. 205–15.

THE PRACTICE OF INCARNATIONAL COMMUNICATION

So far in our discussion of incarnational communication we have focused on the activity of the communicator, who gains the attention of the hearer and identifies with him.

Now let's look at what happens *inside the receiver* as a result of incarnational communication.

Arousing a Need

Much of Jesus' teaching and preaching was intended to arouse a need within His listeners. His approach was more often indirect than direct, but it had the effect of focusing on a need that He knew was already there.

An example of this approach is found in Luke 5. Jesus was sitting inside a house teaching a crowd when a paralyzed man was lowered through the roof and placed in front of Him. Because Jesus knew the *real need* of those gathered, He said to the paralytic, "Man, your sins are forgiven you" (Luke 5:20). This statement not only contained the element of surprise but also pointed dramatically to the essential point Jesus wanted to communicate. But Jesus already knew that His statement would create doubt, not faith, in the minds of those who were skeptics.

Therefore, to further validate His credentials, Jesus identified with the skeptics by asking, "Why are you reasoning in your hearts? Which is easier, to say, 'Your sins are forgiven you,' or to say, 'Rise up and walk?' " (Luke 5:22,23). Knowing their answer would be the former, He demonstrated His power to forgive sins by saying to the paralytic, "I say to you, arise, take up your bed and go to your house" (Luke 5:24). In this instance (and in others like it), Jesus was not pointing primarily to Himself but rather to the human need that lies within. Jesus' action was a visible portrayal that had as its intention the recognition of a need within humanity.

Good communication seeks to arouse a need in the hearer and to offer a way to meet that need.[6] The Christian message deals

[6]For a good discussion of arousing needs, see James Engel, *Contemporary Christian Communications* (Nashville: Thomas Nelson, 1979), p. 112ff.

with man's most basic need: God's forgiveness. Man needs to be healed of the alienation that exists between himself and God. In this sense Jesus met the paralytic's need. He brought forgiveness of sin.

In this incident Jesus met both this basic need and a *felt need*. He dealt with the problem of sin and then quickly turned His attention to the man's physical condition. His interest was in the whole man. This suggests that *if preaching is to be effective it must often be accompanied by a sensitivity toward the physical, mental, and emotional needs of the hearers and a willingness to meet those needs.*

James pointed to this principle when he wrote, "If a brother or sister is naked and destitute of daily food, and one of you says to them, 'Depart in peace, be warmed and filled,' but you do not give them the things which are needed for the body, what does it profit? Thus also faith by itself, if it does not have works, is dead" (James 2:15–17).

The kingdom of Christ is all-inclusive. God's redemption affects the whole man and all of creation. In communicating the gospel we dare not divide the spiritual side of man from the emotional and physical sides as though there were no inter-relatedness among these dimensions. Jesus demonstrated His power in the physical realm; through that the paralytic and others became aware that Jesus had the power to heal in the spiritual realm as well.

Meeting Needs

As we have already said, incarnational communication is aimed at meeting needs. Jesus' concern was often directed toward the poor, the outcast, the blind, and the maimed. He came "not . . . to be served, but to serve, and to give His life a ransom for many" (Mark 10:45). He met both the spiritual and physical needs of people. The attempt to divorce the physical from the spiritual as if they were not related finds no support in the life and ministry of Jesus.[7]

[7]See John Howard Yoder, *The Politics of Jesus* (Grand Rapids: Eerdmans, 1972).

It is important to notice Jesus' strategy for meeting spiritual needs: It was oriented around *self-discovery*. He did not *tell* as much as *show*, and in showing there was usually an element of uncertainty so that the hearer had to come to a recognition of the truth within his own frame of reference and understanding. In general, the Gospels present Jesus in this more "experience-oriented casebook fashion rather than as a predigested theology textbook."[8]

The teaching of Jesus in parables is a good example. When the disciples asked Jesus, "Why do You speak to them in parables?" His answer was "because seeing they do not see, and hearing they do not hear, nor do they understand" (Matt. 13:10,13). He went on to explain that one can hear but not hear, see but not see. What Jesus was alluding to was the condition of the hearer. They do not hear because they do not want to hear. "For the heart of this people has grown dull./Their ears are hard of hearing,/And their eyes they have closed,/Lest they should see with their eyes,/Hear with their ears,/Should understand with their heart,/And should turn,/And I should heal them" (Matt. 13:15). But speaking of His disciples He said, "Blessed are your eyes for they see, and your ears for they hear" (Matt. 13:16).

The point is, nothing is understood unless the hearer makes an effort to understand. Good communication must always take into account the role of the receiver. This does not mean that a communicator may simply "put the material out there" and leave the rest to the hearer. Rather the communicator must realize there are ways to trigger self-discovery.

John the Baptist sent his friends to ask Jesus " 'Are You the Coming One, or do we look for another?' " (Luke 7:20). Jesus did not return a simple yes or no answer. He asked John to decide for himself on the basis of what his disciples had heard and seen. "Go your way," said Jesus, "and tell John the things you have seen and heard: that the blind see, the lame walk, the lepers are cleansed, the deaf hear, the dead are raised, the poor have the gospel preached to them" (Luke 7:22).

[8]Kraft, "The Incarnation," p. 282.

In Christian communication we should not always answer the questions put to us. Rather, we should return the questions to the hearers and demand they decide for themselves. This is a discovery-oriented kind of communication that is not afraid to use visual aids, parables, proverbs, and stories as means through which the hearer may choose to understand what is being said.

CONCLUSION

In the last two chapters an attempt has been made to look at specific ways God has revealed Himself and to draw from those ways some principles for communication. It will be well at this point to reiterate those ideas.

1. God communicates Himself within history.
   - We must speak to man's life in the world.
   - We must communicate God, not simply information about God.
   - God is communicated through *action*. We must become what we communicate.

2. God communicates through language.
   - Language must be appropriate to the context.
   - Language must be related to personal experience.
   - A religious experience is prerequisite to understanding religious truth.
   - A distinction must be made between *essential* religious language and *secondary* religious language.

3. God communicates through vision.
   - Meaning and identity are passed down through images, pictures, and ceremonies.
   - Visual images communicate to the "heart."
   - Visual images must be rooted in truth and expressed in symbols that correspond with the receiver's experience.

4. The ultimate form of God's communication is incarnational.
   - The incarnation contained the attention-getting element.
   - The incarnation contained the identification element.

- Incarnational communication arouses needs.
- Incarnational communication meets needs.

It is not enough to say God has spoken. God has given us the responsibility to communicate Him to the world. In that sense God still speaks. But why is it so difficult to communicate God's message, and why do so many turn away from what seems so clear?

This question is the concern of the next chapter.

7
THE BREAKDOWN: MAN AND SIN

In the last three chapters our questions about the Christian view of communication have revolved around God. In this chapter we turn to man and examine his ability to communicate.

The testimony of Scripture is that man can communicate because he is "a little lower than God" (Ps. 8:4). Man is "fearfully and wonderfully made" (Ps. 139:14). He has been fashioned after the Creator and so, like the Creator, he can communicate.

This Christian view of man is a far cry from the view held by scientism, which states that man is only a complex kind of machine.

Scientism argues that *all* aspects of life—whether the origin of organisms, physical properties, behavior, intelligence, consciousness, or communication are explainable on the basis of principles derived from physical science. The thesis is that a

> single body of natural laws operating on a single set of material particles completely accounts for the origin and properties of living organisms as well as nonliving aggregations of matter and man-made structures. Accordingly, man is essentially no more than a complex machine.[1]

This view regards man's ability to communicate as part of the complex evolutionary process through which man developed his machine-like organisms. In the end however, scientism fails to answer the deeper question of *why* man can communicate.

The biblical answer to the machine allegation is far more satis-

[1] Dean Wooldridge, *Mechanical Man: The Physical Basis of Intelligent Life* (New York: McGraw Hill, 1968), pp. 166–68.

fying. The declaration that man is *a little lower than God* locates the ability of man to communicate in the revolutionary concept that man is made in the image of God.

HUMANITY IN THE IMAGE OF GOD

The root meaning of the word *image* in the Old Testament comes from a Hebrew word that means "to cut." The primary meaning of the word denotes a reproduction or an imitation.

The word was used in the Old Testament to describe the making of idols. Idolaters attempted to cut a facsimile, an exact physical reproduction, of their god; they then fell down and worshiped what had been made. Yahweh forbade the Israelites in the first commandment to "make for yourself an idol, or any likeness of what is in heaven above or on the earth beneath . . ." (Exod. 20:4).

A second way the word *image* is used in the Old Testament has to do with the relationship between a father and son. "Adam," the Book of Genesis tells us, "became the father of a son *in his own likeness, according to his image . . .*" (Gen. 5:3, italics mine). The use of the word here is quite different from the primary use referred to above. The image made out of metal or wood or stone may resemble the original in color, shape, or size. But it is of a *different nature* than the original. However, in the case of Adam's son, the image was of the *same nature* as that of the father. Furthermore, the idol is a *dead* reproduction whereas Adam's son was a *living* reproduction of the father.

There is a third use of the word *image* in the Scripture, and it is this one that we are chiefly concerned with in this chapter.[2] In this case *image* presumes *a relationship between man and God.* "Then God said, 'Let Us make man in Our image, according to Our likeness. . . .' And God created man in His own image, in the image of God He created him; male and female He created them" (Gen. 1:26). The point of this statement is that *man reflects God!*

[2]See Gregory Dom Dix, *The Image and Likeness of God* (New York: Morehouse-Gorham Co., 1954).

While God denies man the right to make and worship any image, God Himself makes man to reflect Himself. In this sense there is a symbol of God in the world—*man*. This peculiar privilege is again referred to in Genesis 6:9: "Whoever sheds man's blood,/By man his blood shall be shed,/For in the image of God/He made man."

A comparison between the second and the third uses of the word *image* points out man's reflection of God more clearly. The Scripture says that Adam *became the father of* a man *who was made in* his own image. However, the son was of the same nature as the father. All humans are alike in terms of their natures.

On the other hand, God *created* man in His own image. Although God's likeness in man is incomparably greater than it is in any other creature, *man is not the same nature with God*. Instead man is the reflection of God. This leaves us with the question: *How does man image or reflect God?*

The Theological Understanding of Image

There is a general consensus among theologians, whether Roman Catholic, Eastern Orthodox, liberal Protestant, or Evangelical, that man reflects God and that the word *image* as used in the Scripture intends to convey this notion.

Irenaeus, an early Eastern church father whose ideas have influenced the development of Eastern Orthodoxy, understood *image* as Adam's reason and freewill and *likeness* as a supernatural endowment through the action of the Spirit. He did not offer the exact meaning of *image* but assumed that man is like a child and must grow into full maturity, becoming more and more like God.[3] The creation of man, then, represents only the beginning of a journey toward full and complete communion with God (or reflection of God).

Since God is Spirit (see John 4:24), it is generally assumed that man's image of God is expressed in spiritual qualities. Several New Testament passages affirm this belief. Paul spoke of putting on the new nature "created according to God, in *righteousness* and true *holiness*" (Eph. 4:24, italics mine). He also wrote of

---

[3]See J.N.D. Kelly, *Early Christian Doctrine* (New York: Harper & Row, 1960), p. 171.

being "renewed in *knowledge* according to the image of Him . . ."
(Col. 3:10, italics mine). In the strictest biblical sense, then,
theologians have agreed that original man was created to reflect
God in *righteousness, holiness,* and *knowledge.*

But theologians have not limited themselves to this more
restrictive approach of defining God's image in man. Throughout
history theologians have sought to discuss man's imaging of God
in a larger and more comprehensive sense. Gregory of Nyssa in
his treatise *On the Creation of Man* finds man's ability to love a
reflection of God's love. "The creator of our nature has also
imparted to us the character of love . . . if love is absent, all the
elements of the image are deformed."[4]

Gordon Kaufman, a modern theologian, seeks for a comprehensive view of man made in the image of God by emphasizing
man's historical nature: "It is important to recognize that it is
man as such, his historical nature, *the totality of his being*, that is
made in God's image, not some attribute or aspect of his being, a
kind of divine element that has been added to his otherwise
animal nature."[5]

For example, the very creation of culture by man, which in
itself is intrinsic to man's historical character, is a way of imaging
God's creation of the world. The word *image* cannot be limited,
therefore, to refer to the spiritual aspect of man. Instead it points
to the very heart of what man is all about. Man is able, to a certain
extent, to shape history and to determine the outcome of personal
and world events precisely because he is made in the image of
God. In this sense everything that man is (sin excepted) points in
an analogical way to God.

Using this line of argument, it is appropriate to say that one of
the ways in which man is analogous to God is in his ability to
communicate. The triune God, in whom we find eternal communication, has made man in such a way that *he* reflects the gift of
communication.

Another approach that theologians have taken toward man

[4]Quoted in John Meyendorff, *Byzantine Theology* (New York: Fordham University
Press, 1974), p. 138.
[5]Gordon D. Kaufman, *Systematic Theology* (New York: Scribner, 1969).

made in the image of God is the christological method. Paul speaks of Christ as the "image of the invisible God" (Col. 1:15). The witness of Scripture is that God "became flesh," thereby bearing His image in the incarnate Christ. God then gave us an example in Christ of what it means to be fully human. Jesus is not only the Savior who died to save us from sin but also the perfect reflection of what God is like.

For this reason the apostles encouraged Christians to imitate Jesus: "Be kind to one another, tenderhearted, forgiving one another, just as God in Christ also has forgiven you" (Eph. 4:32); "Let this mind be in you which was also in Christ Jesus" (Phil. 2:5). By *exemplifying* Christ in one's life by way of imitation, the Christian is able to show forth God: "Let your light so shine before men, that they may see your good works and glorify your Father who is in heaven" (Matt. 5:16).[6]

When I talk about man made in the image of God, I am talking about communication. God communicates Himself by placing an *imprint* of Himself on man. The perfect imprint of God is found in Jesus. Those who belong to Christ are called upon to imitate Jesus, thereby demonstrating the reality of God. In this way man by his very life communicates God.

A Theocentric View of Man

The biblical view of man is obviously theocentric. The central theme of Scriptures about man is that his nature is not a static or "closed" entity. Instead, man is an "open" and dynamic being whose very essence is determined by his relationship with God. The question "Why does man communicate?" cannot be answered apart from a recognition of man's theocentric character. God communicates love within Himself among His three Persons, Father, Son, and Holy Spirit. His creatures are not an extension of Himself, but they bear His stamp. They reflect the personality of the Creator. Thus, Gregory of Nazianzen wrote, "Man was set

[6]For a thorough treatment of this notion and for the entire concept of man in the image of God, see Cornelius G. Berkhouwer, *Man: The Image of God*, trans. Dirk W. Zellma (Grand Rapids: Eerdmans, 1962), especially ch. 3.

upon the earth as a kind of second world, a microcosm."[7] In the East to this day, man is called God's *icon*.

A brief examination of the biblical account of man in the Garden suggests that man enjoyed the ability to communicate on four levels: He was in communication with *God*, with *himself*, with his *fellowman*, and with *nature*. The implication of the Genesis story is that original man was in a paradise situation that Western theologians refer to as a time of man's perfection. An important observation for our purpose is to recognize that *when man is in fellowship and communication with God, all areas in which he functions as a communicating being are in balance*. God made man in His image. When man images God and functions as he was made to function, he gives glory to God. This is no less true in the area of communication than in any other aspect in which man images his Creator.

Implications

The Christian teaching that man is made in the image of God and therefore bears the stamp of the Creator contains a number of inferences for a theology of communication.

In the first place, *man is a reflection of God*. If, as we have already argued, communication in the Godhead is an intrinsic part of God, then we can deduce that man's ability to communicate is a reflection of the Creator's ability. Man, one may say, is born with the innate ability to communicate. The ability to speak and symbolize meaning is not derived from the adaptation of evolving organisms to external challenges, as scientific materialism suggests. Rather, it rests on the divine creative act of God who made man in His image. Science may be helpful in describing the technical aspects of human communication, but science cannot tell us *why* we have this ability.

Second, *the true meaning of communication is best realized when man communicates with God*. A theocentric view of man realizes man's true nature lends itself not to autonomy but to

---

[7]See Henry Bettenson, *The Later Christian Fathers* (New York: Oxford University Press, 1972), p. 101.

relationship. Because man's real purpose is fulfilled through a relationship with God, his role in the world will be best lived as he allows the image of God to be reflected through him. The closer, therefore, man is to God the better the communication both between God and man and then between man and himself, his neighbor, and nature.

Third, *the image of God in man necessarily means that man has a special task in the world.* As man opens himself to God, he begins to relate differently with God's creation. God's visible world has been declared good. As the image of God, man is lord of creation. His communion with God is not a supra-historical event but one that occurs in time, space, and history.

For this reason true communication is not only directed toward the Creator but also toward the creation. Man is both of God and of the dust of the ground. His communication or reflection of God to the world is an important aspect of what it means to be a communicating creature. Adam named the animals, was given dominion over the earth, and was commanded to cultivate and maintain the earth. One of his functions in the world was that of communicator between God and His creation.

After the fall, this task became more demanding. Polarities entered into life and history. Saint Maximus, in a famous passage in his work *Ambigua 41,* mentioned five polarities (creating barriers in communication) that man has to overcome: (1) God and creation, (2) the intelligible (rational) and the sensible (sensory), (3) heaven and earth, (4) paradise and world, (5) man and woman. These polarities have been made greater by sin and are, therefore, insurmountable by man alone. Only the man Christ Jesus, who is the *full* image of God, has been able to overcome them. He is the Second Adam, and in Him creation began again.[8]

The calling of the Christian communicator is, therefore, to be united with God through Jesus Christ and to speak to the polarities of the world in the name and the power of Jesus. This task and function is fulfilled only through Jesus Christ, the true image of God, who has made all things new. Man is called to conform to the image of Christ and to preach and declare to the

[8]Quoted in John Meyendorff, *Byzantine Theology,* p. 143.

world the message of ultimate meaning through communication with God in Jesus Christ.

Fourth, a conditional factor to keep in mind is that *man is not forced to be in communion with God.* Man's choice to relate or not to relate to his Creator has much to do with the question of communication. Sin has caused the breakdown of communication in the world, and man's refusal to overcome sin through Jesus Christ has created barriers to communication. A theology of communication cannot overlook this insight, which bears significance for a Christian understanding of the task of communication.

THE BREAKDOWN OF COMMUNICATION

The Genesis account quickly moves from the description of man's original relationship with God in the Garden to the rebellion of man against God. The story of Genesis 3 explains the religious significance of man's rejection of the lordship of God over his life. Man chose to obey and follow Satan rather than God. The consequence of this choice was a loss of communication between himself and God—a loss that also affects his communication with himself, with his fellowman, and with nature.

The Breakdown of Communication Between Man and God

After Adam and Eve had both eaten of the tree of the knowedge of good and evil, they "hid themselves from the presence of the LORD . . ." (Gen. 3:8). Their sin broke down the communion they had enjoyed with God. They had set someone else in God's place, and now they wanted to run from God and hide. They had a secret that pushed them away from God, created a barrier of fear, and resulted in excuses and accusations in an attempt to cover up this shift of loyalties. The account ends with a statement of separation:

Therefore the LORD God sent him forth from the garden of Eden, to cultivate the ground from which he was taken. So He drove the man out; and at the east of the garden of Eden He stationed the cherubim, and the flaming sword which turned every direction, to guard the way to the tree of life (Gen. 3:23,24).

What happened to Adam affected the whole human race. Paul interpreted the event in this way: "Therefore as by one man sin entered into the world, and death by sin, and thus death spread to all men, because all sinned" (Rom. 5:12). Paul applied this principle to the whole *history* of man. The break between man and God was a spiritual break that had consequences in the physical, material realm of man's life as well.

In the opening chapter of Romans, Paul set this historical principle before the Roman people. The history of man is a history of *suppressing the truth*. Even though God can be known through the creation, men "did not glorify Him as God, nor were thankful . . ." (Rom. 1:21). Instead they "became futile in their thoughts" (Rom. 1:21), and they "exchanged the truth of God for the lie, and worshiped and served the creature rather than the Creator . . ." (Rom. 1:25). For this reason "God gave them up . . ." (Rom. 1:26). By this Paul means that God gave them *over* to their own sin. He let man go his way.

The result of man's going his own way has been "all unrighteousness, sexual immorality, wickedness, covetousness, maliciousness; full of envy, murder, strife, deceit, evil-mindedness; they are whisperers, backbiters, haters of God, violent, proud, boasters, inventors of evil things, disobedient to parents, undiscerning, untrustworthy, unloving, unforgiving, unmerciful" (Rom. 1:29–31).

The point Paul made is that the break with God by Adam set in motion a chain of events in the life of the world that has affected man in every area of his life. Man has distorted and defaced the image in which he was created, and thus communication as part of that image is not carried on as originally intended.

The Breakdown of Communication With Self

One of the specific results of man's breakdown in communication with God is that *man no longer truly communicates with himself.* Augustine spoke to this aspect of man in his *Confessions.* "For thou madest us for thyself, and our heart is restless, until it repose in thee."[9]

---

[9]Aurelius Augustine, *Confessions* (Mt. Vernon: Peter Pauper Press, n.d.), book 1, p. 9.

The story of Cain provides the first concrete biblical example of this principle. After Cain killed his brother Abel, God declared, ". . . you shall be a vagrant and a wanderer on the earth" (Gen. 4:12). A vagrant and a wanderer is someone who is not only separated from something or someone external to himself, but one who is also alienated from himself. When Cain "went out from the presence of the LORD" (Gen. 4:16), he began a long search for meaning.

The biblical record suggests that he sought meaning by building a city and by having a son. But the story of Cain is one of a man whose life is characterized by restlessness, wandering, and searching. As French educator and Christian philosopher Jacques Ellul suggests, "It is God's absence which is the never-ending sting planted in his heart . . . the search for home, the search for Eden, is in the end a constant desire for God's presence."[10]

All mankind, like Cain, is aware of the loss of the presence of God and therefore of their own incompleteness. Humans do not know the true meaning of their existence and therefore cast about for something or someone in whom to find personal meaning and security.

The estrangement from self really begins with the assertion of self. Because man was made by God and for God, the refusal to accept this relationship leads man into making *himself* or some other aspect of the created order his god.

Because man turns to self in an autonomous way, man does not truly understand self or the importance of a relationship with the Creator that defines the meaning of self and clarifies the function of the self in the world. Instead man elevates himself and thus becomes selfish. He sees himself as an end and therefore becomes demanding. Orienting his life toward himself, whether through pleasure, power, sex, wealth, or any other number of self-oriented pursuits, he cuts himself off from his true self-understanding and destiny in the world.

Consequently, a breakdown occurs in the inner man, and thus a true assessment of the self cannot be made. The meaning of his

[10]Jacques Ellul, *The Meaning of the City* (Grand Rapids: Eerdmans, 1970), p. 4.

existence and work has been severed from true understanding. He finds a substitute in the elevation of self and in the finite realities of life at hand. But they are substitutes that do not answer his deepest needs. For until he knows God, he does not know himself and the true meaning of his life in the world.

The Breakdown of Communication Among People

The loss of communication between man and God not only affects man's relationship with himself but also creates a breakdown of communication among people in society at large.

Because man is the agent of cultural unfolding, it is only natural that the whole sweep of human history reflects the character of man. Man unfolds culture in such a way that culture reveals and enlarges man's self-alienation. The personal departure of man from God and His will becomes magnified in the collective witness of man's life in society. Society is made up of men who are wanderers and vagabonds. Together they create societies and cultures that reflect this collective search for meaning as well as the collective evil such a search creates when it moves "away from the presence of God."[11]

The above interpretation seems to be the religious meaning of the flood. The alienation from God that was first experienced by Adam and then passed down to succeeding generations resulted in a society that can only be described in the following terms: "Then the LORD saw that the wickedness of man was great on the earth, and that every intent of the thoughts of his heart was only evil continually" (Gen. 6:5).

Sin creates a destructive movement, a *dynamic* force that separates not only persons, but whole societies, even the whole of humanity, from the original meaning and purpose of life—communion with God both through a relationship with God and through the fulfillment of man's task and function in the world. Here we have a vivid picture of the ruination of man's work in the world as a result of man's falling away from God. As the history of

[11]This theme is developed in Robert Webber, *The Secular Saint* (Grand Rapids: Zondervan, 1979).

sin unfolds, God's image in man is subjected to a continuous process of destruction.

This self-perpetuating destruction expresses itself in the social dimension of existence as much as it does in the individual life. Sin has unleashed the demonic powers that Paul labeled "principalities," "powers," "rulers of the darkness of this age," "spiritual wickedness in the heavenly places" (Eph. 6:12).

These powers seek to persuade man that he is, after all, autonomous. He does not need God. He can build his own life without God. This attitude of independence lies at the heart of the ancient story of the tower of Babel. The theme of this event is not "reaching God" but building an ultimate statement to the glory and independence of man. " 'Come, let us build for ourselves a city, and a tower whose top will reach into heaven, and *let us make for ourselves a name*, lest we be scattered abroad over the face of the whole earth' " (Gen. 11:4, italics mine). Man thought he could master the powers of nature and be free from the authority of God. But the confusion of language that halted the project of man's self-glory demonstrated the power of God over all attempts to create a meaningful world without Him.

The history of the world points to repeated attempts between men and nations of men to create unity, establish peace, and live as brothers. While these efforts do sometimes result in short-term successes, they all ultimately go the way of the tower of Babel. Man cannot by himself break down the historical, cultural, and political barriers that stand in the way of all peoples' being in communion with each other.

The Breakdown of Communication Between Man and Nature

There is a curious reference to "the ground" that runs through the Genesis account. In the curses of God against man in Genesis 3, He said,

Cursed is the ground because of you;
In toil you shall eat of it
All the days of your life.
Both thorns and thistles it shall grow for you;
And you shall eat the plants of the field;

By the sweat of your face
You shall eat bread,
Till you return to the ground,
Because from it you were taken;
For you are dust,
And to dust you shall return (Gen. 3:17–20).

In the curse against Cain God said, "And now you are cursed from the ground . . ." (Gen. 4:11); Cain in response to God said, "Behold, Thou hast driven me this day from the face of the ground . . ." (Gen. 4:14). These Scriptures have generally been recognized, especially by the Eastern church fathers, as statements that refer to the *suffering of nature* as a result of the fall.

God had initially intended to communicate Himself through nature. Nature was to speak clearly and forcibly of God's special relationship with it. Although God can still speak through nature, the clarity of His presence has been obscured. Because man the "microcosm" was given control over nature, his choice to serve Satan rather than God opened the creation up to the service of the evil one. Creation does not belong to Satan, but it has become the arena in which he exercises his authority over man. It has become the domain and the instrument of Satan. In this sense the creation is also alienated from God and man as well as from the original purpose and meaning that God intended for the creation.

Implications of Sin for Communication

Sin's effect on communication has *cosmic significance*. If the fall can be described (as it is described in the Scriptures) as a breakdown in communion (or communication) between God and His entire created order, then the problem of communication is crucial.

There is, one may say, a cosmic tension at the very center of life that will only be resolved when creation is united again to God through Jesus Christ. Paul referred to this cosmic tension in his letter to the Ephesians. He spoke of Christians who once followed "the course of this world, according to the prince of the power of the air, the spirit who now works in the sons of disobedience"

(Eph. 2:2). They "once conducted [themselves] in the lusts of [their] flesh, fulfilling the desires of the flesh and of the mind, and were by nature chidren of wrath, just as the others" (Eph. 2:3). But then they were made "alive together with Christ" and were seated with Him "in the heavenly places" (Eph. 2:5,6).

Because of this action of God in Christ, He "has broken down the middle wall of division" and has reconciled us "both to God in one body by the cross, by it having put to death the enmity" (Eph. 2:14,16). In Jesus Christ, God has broken down all the communication barriers in the entire cosmic order. The Christian now anticipates the fulfillment of God's cosmic work. In the meantime his calling in the world has to do with the realization of the eschatalogical goal in the here and now.

The task of communication, to be biblical, must always be viewed in the light of the ultimate reconciliation of broken communication. For this reason a Christian communicator is both a realist and an optimist. As a realist he knows that barriers to communication exist. As an optimist he knows Christ has already united all polarities in Himself and that they will be finally resolved at the consummation.

The effects of sin on communication also have *personal significance*. A unique characteristic of the biblical doctrine of sin is that it includes within its perspective both the personal and the cosmic. Man's decision to move in a direction away from God is personal but not individualistic. An individualistic approach to sin assumes that sin affects only the person.

The testimony of Scripture is that each person in the world participates in the breakdown of communication with God, himself, his neighbor, and nature. Christ's work of reconciliation, then, must be applied to each individual on a personal level. A Christian communicator must take seriously his own participation in the breakdown of communication as well as that of the persons with whom he communicates.

Finally, *the cosmic and personal ramifications of the breakdown of communication are expressed in the social order.* In this sense we may say the effects of sin on communication have *social significance*. By nature man is truly man when living in company with others. This fellowship of man is chiefly expressed in marriage, in the family, in working relationships, and supremely in the church.

In each case these sets of relationships represent the God-ordained task and function of man in the world. Because man has turned from God, he has distorted himself, set off a chain of cosmic broken relationships, and changed the nature of social relationships. Because man has acted as tyrant in his social relationships and has sought to be the ruler in his relationships rather than the servant, he has created an abnormal society.

It was God's original intention to create a society in which relationships would be modeled by the Trinitarian unity. Instead, man, because of his rebellion, has created a culture in which communication within marriage, the family, and work are in disarray. The restoration of communication, therefore, looks to a new society, the church, where relationships between couples, in families, and in work are restored.[12]

CONCLUSION

In this chapter we have attempted to deal with the subject of man and the breakdown of communication. These are the major points that have been made:

- Man is made in the image of the triune God.
- The *image* is reflected in the totality of man's life in the world. It is not limited to spiritual qualities but has to do with his *task* and *function* in the world.
- The purpose of man in the world is best fulfilled as he allows the image of God to be fulfilled through him, both in his spiritual qualities and in his task and function in the world.
- Because man has broken his relationship with God, the *image* within him has become distorted.

[12]The ideas in this paragraph are treated more fully in André Bieler, *The Social Humanism of Calvin* (Richmond: John Knox Press, 1964), p. 9ff.

- This perversion of the *image* results in broken communication in every area of man's life—with himself, with his fellowman, and with nature.

- The implications of the Christian teaching about man for communication theory are far-reaching. They extend into the entire cosmos, touch each person, and affect all human relationships.

8
THE RESTORATION: CHRIST AND REDEMPTION

In the last chapter I pointed to the breakdown of communication caused by one's choice to sin against God.

In this chapter I want to look at the *restoration of communication*. The breakdown of communication is associated with one man, Adam, and the effect that his sin had and continues to have on the whole human race. Likewise the restoration of communication focuses on one Man, Christ, and the effect He has had and continues to have on the whole human race.

The argument of this chapter is that Christ, the new Man, restored everything that was lost as a result of Adam's sin. Secondly, I argue for a community of restored people (the church) as that social unit from which the healing of communication breakdown radiates to the whole world.

CHRIST: THE RESTORER OF COMMUNICATION

As Adam failed to accomplish his purpose and so plunged the whole created order into sin (thus causing the breakdown of communication), so the Second Adam reversed the human situation (thus restoring communication).

Christ: The New Man

We begin our study with the recognition that the One who restores communication is both man and God. The Christian christological confession affirms that Jesus is both the image of God and the perfect image of man.

Jesus is God. The author of Hebrews wrote, "He . . . being the brightness of His [God's] glory and the express image of His [God's] person . . ." (Heb. 1:3). The relationship of the Son to the

Father was discussed at the Nicene Council (A.D. 325). In this council the church affirmed the unity of the Son with the Father and confessed that Jesus is "God of very God." His relationship to the Father was described as one of generation, not creation. The Father created the world out of nothing but *begat* the Son from His very essence. Therefore, Christian theology confesses the Son to be of the same substance and essence with the Father. He is the perfect image of God.

Jesus is Man. John wrote, "the Word *became flesh* and dwelt among us" (John 1:14, italics mine). We know from the Gospels that Jesus was of human lineage. The salutation to Mary by Gabriel affirms the humanity of Jesus: "And behold, you will conceive in your womb and bring forth a Son, and shall call His name JESUS" (Luke 1:31). John later insisted that those who do not confess Jesus *in the flesh* are anti-Christ and do not belong to God (see 1 John 4:2,3). A major controversy of the early church ended with the affirmation of the full humanity of Jesus. The Chalcedonian Definition (A.D. 451) stated that Jesus was "consubstantial with us in manhood." In that Jesus was fully man, He shared the human image of man in which Adam and all other people have been created.

Paul brought together the two natures of Jesus in the salutation to the Romans: ". . . Jesus Christ our Lord, who was born of the seed of David *according to the flesh* and declared to be the Son of God with power, *according to the Spirit* of holiness, by the resurrection from the dead" (Rom. 1:3, 4, italics mine).

Jesus is therefore in a unique position to restore communication. Communication is restored by God through Man. Only Jesus is fully God and fully Man. Only Jesus can restore communication.

Christ Recapitulates the Old

The Christian view of *restored communication* is based on the poetic imagery of the first and Second Adam motif. As the first Adam did something *to* the human race, so the Second Adam did something *for* the human race. The first Adam brought sin, death, and condemnation, but the Second Adam reversed this and brought righteousness, life, and justification (see Rom. 5:12–21). And, as we all bear the image of the first Adam, so also we may bear the image of the Second Adam: "As we have borne the image of the man of dust, we shall also bear the image of the heavenly Man" (1 Cor. 15:49).

The meaning of Paul's contrast between the first and second Adams was understood by the early Fathers of the church in relation to the atonement and the theology of recapitulation. Iranaeus (A.D. 180), one of the first Fathers to expand this theme, put it this way:

> So the Lord now manifestly came to his own, and born by his own created order which he himself bears, *he by his obedience on the tree renewed (and reversed) what was done by disobedience in connection with a tree;* . . . Then indeed the sin of the first-formed man was amended by the chastisement of the First-begotten, the wisdom of the serpent was conquered by the simplicity of the dove, and the chains were broken by which we were in bondage to death.
>
> Therefore he renews these things in himself, uniting man to the Spirit; and placing the Spirit in man, he himself is made the head of the Spirit, and gives the Spirit to be the head of man, for by him we see and hear and speak.
>
> He therefore completely renewed all things, both taking up the battle against our enemy, and crushing him who at the beginning had led us captive in Adam, trampling on his head, as you find in Genesis that God said to the serpent, "And I will put enmity between you and the woman, and between your seed and her seed; he will be on the watch for your head, and you will be on the watch for his heel" (italics mine).[1]

This theology of recapitulation is rooted in the New Testament teaching that Jesus Christ is the image of God and the image of man. It was expressed in two axioms developed within the consciousness of the ancient church and articulated by the church fathers as they worked out a New Testament theology of salvation.

The first axiom is "only God can save." From this perspective

[1] Irenaeus, "Against Heresies," *Early Christian Fathers,* ed. Cyril Richardson (Philadelphia: Westminster Press, 1953), book 2, ss. 2 and 19, pp. 389–90.

we recognize the gap in communication between God and the creation to be of such a nature that only God himself, not a man, can breach the gulf. In this the New Testament agrees—Jesus Christ is fully God.

The second axiom is "only that which is assumed is healed." This axiom stresses the necessity that man's savior be a man. Only man can fully participate in what it means to be man. Only man can experience the brokenness of the shattered relationship between man and God and the consequences it effects in man and his relationships with others and with nature. Jesus was fully man, as the New Testament records, and thus fully identified with man and his condition. The term *Second Adam* refers to and affirms the humanity of Jesus.

The Cosmic Significance of Jesus' Work

The image of the Second Adam brings out the *cosmic significance* of Jesus. The sin of the first man bore cosmic results by initiating a chain of events that destroyed man's relationship with the entire created order. The righteous obedience of the Second Adam, however, reversed that order of events and brought *potential healing* to all those broken relationships.

Paul referred to the cosmic effect of Jesus in his letter to the Colossian Christians: "For it pleased the Father that in Him all fullness should dwell, and by Him to reconcile *all things* [including communications] to Himself . . . whether things on earth or things in heaven, having made peace through the blood of His cross" (Col. 1:19,20, italics mine). In this passage Paul connected the incarnation with creation and redemption. The One who effected the reconciliation is "the image of the invisible God, the first-born over all creation," the One by whom "all things were created" and in whom "all things hold together" (Col. 1:15,16,17). The cosmic reality is that the Creator Himself has entered into the creation that He might save it and bring healing to the broken relationships that characterize its fallenness. No wonder Paul could write with exaltation: "For of Him and through Him and to Him are all things, to whom be glory forever. Amen" (Rom. 11:36).

The early church expressed the wonder of this theme in her early hymns:

> Man fell from the divine and better life; though made in the image of God, through transgression he became wholly subject to corruption and decay. But now the wise creator fashions him anew; for he has been glorified.[2]

> David foreseeing in spirit the sojourn with men of the only begotten Son in the flesh, called the creation to rejoice with him, and prophetically lifted up his voice to cry: "Tabor and Herman shall rejoice in my name" [Ps. 88:13]. For having gone up, O Christ, with thy disciples into Mount Tabor, thou wast transfigured, and hast made the nature that had grown dark in Adam to shine again as lightening.[3]

The Historical Significance of the Work of Christ

Not only does Christ's work parallel Adam's in its cosmic significance, but also in its *historical* significance. As Adam's sin initiated a chain of events that affected history, so Christ's death and resurrection set in motion a chain of events that take shape in history.

We have already seen that by nature man is an historical being. The *Imago* (the image of God in man) is expressed in history in the task and function of man and in the relationships man sustains in marriage, family, and work. Because man is a social creature, and because man has by his sin perverted his social relationships, it follows that man's redemption must take place in history in the context of his God-ordained task and human relationships. It is here, in life itself, where man's broken communication is expressed. *It must be here, in life itself, where man's restored communication is expressed.*

The historical nature of reconciliation is the fundamental theme of the Old Testament. Man *in his history* is called to return

---

[2]December 25, Matins; *The Festal Menaion*, trans. Mother Mary and K. Ware (London: Faber, 1969), p. 254. Quoted in John Meyendorff, *Byzantine Theology* (New York: Fordham University Press, 1974), p. 152.
[3]August 6, Transfiguration, Vespers; *Festal Menaion*, pp. 476–77. Quoted in Meyendorff, *Byzantine Theology*, p. 152.

to obedience to the will of God and to full communion with God and to all that such a relationship represents.

The first dramatic move in this direction was made by the call of God to Abraham. He was to go out "not knowing where he was going" (Heb. 11:8). *His obedient response* was a demonstration of his willingness to make a move toward the will of God leaving behind his own personal desires and longings. In this we see the potential reversal of Adam's selfishness.

The second important historical event in which the movement toward the kingdom may be seen is in the exodus event. At Mount Sinai God entered into an agreement with a *people* who agreed " 'All that the LORD has spoken we will do, and we will be obedient' " (Exod. 24:7). Here, loyalty toward God as well as the establishment of a personal relationship between God and man became apparent. Man had committed himself *in community* to fulfill the purposes of God and to establish an historical witness to the relationship that can exist between man and God.

This movement on the part of man (failure not withstanding) led man to the recognition of God as absolute Lord of all history. The whole movement of history was seen by the prophets as the working out of the personal purposes of God. God was moving His people toward the establishment of the kingdom of righteousness. This kingdom, which was to come out of the loins of David (see 2 Sam. 7:12–17), would extend into the whole world (see Isa. 66).

This vision of a future historical kingdom was alive in the New Testament period. Jesus came preaching, "The time is fulfilled, and the kingdom of God is at hand. Repent and believe in the gospel" (Mark 1:15). Jesus pointed to the beginning of the kingdom in Himself. That is, in the historical incarnation of God the Son in Jesus Christ, and by His death and resurrection, the polarities that separate man from God and man from Himself, His neighbor, and nature have been overcome. Jesus has defeated Satan and all his power "having wiped out the handwriting of requirements that was against us, which was contrary to us. And He has taken it out of the way, having nailed it to His cross. Having disarmed principalities and powers, He made a public spectacle of them, triumphing over them in it" (Col. 2:14,15).

The kingdom is the establishment of God's reign *on earth* where a visible and tangible manifestation of an entire created order in communion with its Creator will be manifested. This kingdom has not yet come (see Rev. 20), but the witness to the kingdom and an instrument of the kingdom has been established—the church. And it is here, in the church, where the presence of the future kingdom is to be found.[4] *It is here, in the church, where communion with God has been restored and where the source for the potential healing of the breakdown of communication within God's creation is found.*

CHURCH: THE COMMUNITY OF RESTORED COMMUNICATION

The atonement holds the key to the restoration of broken communication. The consequences of Christ's victory over death are twofold. First, Christ *broke the power of evil* that holds sway over the lives of people and perpetuates the breakdown of communication in every area of life. Second, people need no longer live in bondage to sin, but are now *free to live in genuine community* with God and fellow believers in the life of the church.

The work of Christ was cosmic in that it represented a new beginning. Paul wrote to the Corinthians that "old things have passed away; behold, all things have become new" (2 Cor. 5:17). In the atonement the world's opportunity to acknowledge God's sovereignty was being re-established, and the possibility of a new and genuine life for man was made available. Jesus had come that "they may have life, and that they may have it more abundantly" (John 10:10). What Jesus gave was an opportunity for people to be servants to one another (see Gal. 5:13).

The context in which this restored communication is to take place, however, is not in some nebulous and ethereal sphere, but in the church.[5] The church is the people of God *on earth*. It is the visible, tangible, historical, and social body of people who belong to Christ. These are the people who are related to God and to the

---

[4]See George Eldon Ladd, *The Presence of the Future* (Grand Rapids: Eerdmans, 1974).
[5]See James F. Engel, *Contemporary Christian Communications* (Nashville: Thomas Nelson, 1979), p. 89ff.

world in a new way. Therefore, it is in the context of the household of God, the church, where restored communication must begin. This perspective contains numerous implications for our method of communication. But before we can look more closely at the implications, we need to get a clearer picture of the church as the *locus* of restored communication.

Restored Communication in the Church

Just as Adam was made in the image of God and given a task and function in the world, so those who are in Christ are re-made in the image of God and given a task and function as citizens of the new creation, the church.

An understanding of the major New Testament images of the church gives us a clearer picture of the concrete context in which the new man is called to express his restored communication. These images are four: the people of God; the new creation; the fellowship in faith; and the body.[6]

The image of the church as *the people of God* (see 1 Cor. 1:2) has a twofold emphasis. First, the work of God in Jesus Christ, who created and called the church into being, is of primary importance. The church is not a collection of people who come together of their own volition; rather God has called or recalled to Himself those who are the church. Second, the church is not a static institution but a dynamic community of people who are related to each other in a new way.

The new way in which the people of God are related to one another is captured in the second image, *the new creation*. Already we have seen that Christ initiated something new. That something is not a new teaching, a new moral order, or a new utopian vision. It is deeper and more radical than any of these. What is new is the beginning again of creation in the church. The kingdom has been inaugurated and is now beginning to spread throughout the world. A new relationship with the fallen creation has been established in Jesus Christ. This new beginning set

---

[6]For an expanded treatment of these images, see Paul Minear, *Images of the Church in the New Testament* (Philadelphia: Westminster Press, 1960).

forth a chain of events that will culminate in the new heavens and the new earth.

The emphasis on the future, however, does not diminish the visibility of the church in the world. Rather, the third image, *the fellowship in faith,* describes that fabric of human relationships which the new creation establishes. We are called in the church to be servants of one another. "For we do not preach ourselves, but Christ Jesus the Lord, and ourselves your servants for Jesus' sake" (2 Cor. 4:5). Within the context of this commitment, man can no longer be a tyrant over his fellowman. On the horizontal level our transformed relationships are service-oriented.

The image that most fittingly describes these new relationships is that of *the body.* It brings all the other images of the church together and expresses the incarnational dimension of the church. Because the church is in indissoluble union with Christ and the Holy Spirit, the ministry of Christ continues in the church, His body, by the action of the Holy Spirit. The church is therefore the center of the world from which and through which God's work of reconciliation, and thus the restoration of communication, must radiate.

This emphasis on the church as the locus of restored communication means there is a community of people on earth that experience (or at least are called to experience) the new reality of restored communication. The effective Christian communicator, then, must communicate from within the context of that new community of people. It is not enough to speak about the message, the message must be lived!

Just as there are effects of what the first Adam did *to* man and the created order, so there are effects of what the Second Adam does *for* man and the created order. Specifically, just as Adam's sin and the subsequent sin of the human race destroyed communication between man and God and affected man's relationship with himself, his fellow man, and nature, so Christ's work and the church as the extension of Himself in the world repairs and restores man's communication in all these areas. (Although, as noted above, the full and complete restoration of creation to its original glory awaits the consummation.) Thus the experience of restored communication in the church finds itself in the tension between what is and what is to come. We must look at restored communication, therefore, both from the point of view of God and the point of view of the church on earth.

In the first place, *communication with God is restored by Christ and experienced in the church.* At the conclusion of Paul's discussion of the comparison between the first and Second Adam in Romans 5, he fittingly wrote "so that as sin has reigned in death, even so grace might reign through righteousness to eternal life by Jesus Christ our Lord" (Rom. 5:21). It is most fitting, and a matter of theological interest, that Paul moved from this great passage on justification into a discussion on baptism in Romans 6.

Baptism is the passage rite into the body of Christ, the church. Anyone who has been justified by faith and has, as Paul stated in Romans 5:1, "peace with God through our Lord Jesus Christ" is now called to an identification with Christ through a baptism "into His death" (Rom. 6:3). Baptism, especially by immersion, is a powerful material symbol of what actually happens when communication with God is restored.[7] It is the material symbol of our spiritual union with Christ as Paul says, "For if we have been united together in the likeness of His death, certainly we also shall be in the likeness of His resurrection" (Rom. 6:5).

When Jesus commanded His disciples to " 'Go therefore and make disciples of all the nations, *baptizing* them in the name of the Father and of the Son and of the Holy Spirit' " (Matt. 28:19, italics mine), He had in mind that indissoluble union between Himself and the church that is expressed in restored communication. This is born out by His concluding statement: " '. . . and behold, I am with you always, even to the end of the age' " (Matt. 28:20). God's presence is both personal and corporate in the church. The life of the believer is lived out in the context of the church, Christ's body, to which he belongs. Thus, the statement of Cyprian (A.D. 250) that "he who has not the church for his mother has not God for his father" stands.

The point in which the church most clearly demonstrates this

[7]See Peter E. Gillquist, *The Physical Side of Being Spiritual* (Grand Rapids: Zondervan, 1979), ch. 8.

restored communication is in the Eucharist. The early church approached the Eucharist as the key to ecclesiology. As John Meyendorff comments,

> the church, for them, was primarily the place where God and man met in the Eucharist, and the Eucharist became the criterion of ecclesial structure and the inspiration of all Christian action and responsibility in the world. In both cases the Eucharist was understood in a cosmological and ecclesiological dimension affirmed in the formula of the Byzantine oblation: "Thine own of thine own, we offer unto thee in behalf of all and for all."[8]

The Eucharist is the material symbol of our spiritual communion with Christ, and through His death and resurrection communication with God is restored. The kingdom of God is therefore made *present* to us in the Eucharist as well as prophetically anticipated. Thus, the Eucharist brings together creation, incarnation, atonement, and consummation in the church in restored communication. Consequently the Eucharist is not something to be "looked upon"; rather it is a powerful action of the Holy Spirit whereby the very kingdom represented is meant to be realized in the church through the action of the Holy Spirit.

The second way *communication is restored in the church is through the acceptance of self.* Just as the entrance of sin alienated man from himself (as seen in Cain) and produced within man those self-destroying habits of sin described by Paul (see Gal. 5:19–21), so reconciliation with God through Christ brings substantial healing to a person's experience of self.

The love of self is related to what psychologist Carl Rogers calls "the internal frame of reference."[9] It has to do with the sum total of the ways in which a person sees, feels, evaluates, and organizes his world of experience. One who is in Christ, and therefore in the church, wears a new set of glasses. He sees himself and his world from a different perspective.

Man's self-worth is derived not from anything he has done but

---

[8]Meyendorff, *Byzantine Theology* p. 207.
[9]Carl R. Rogers, *Client-Centered Therapy* (Boston: Houghton Mifflin, 1951), p. 29.

from the realization that he is remade in the image of God. Paul spoke of the Christian as "renewed in the spirit of your mind," and called on him "to put on the new man, created according to God, in righteousness and true holiness" (Eph. 4:23,24). Also there is a restored sense of the task and function of man in the world. Man no longer sees himself as a mere cog in the machine or a cork tossed about on the ocean, but instead he regards himself in relation to his calling in life. His self-acceptance is rooted in a recognition of the part he is to play in the drama of creation and redemption.

But this self-realization does not take place in a vacuum. Rather, it comes to fruition in the church, the body of Christ. Paul wrote of the varieties of "gifts," "ministries," and "activities" that are given for "mutual profit" (1 Cor. 12:4–7). What Paul was expressing here, and throughout 1 Corinthians 12–14, is the principle that each person is to be accepted for the gifts he brings to the community. This points to the principle of self-acceptance that is basic to the Christian attitude toward self. It does not deny growth, whether emotional or spiritual. Rather, it affirms growth and recognizes that not all Christians are at the same level. This means that tolerance toward each other in the church is a necessary prerequisite for growth.

Again, the Eucharist is the focal point for the healing of the self. It locates and symbolizes the action of God in Christ through which man (because of the incarnation) has been united to God. This union of God and man proclaimed in the Eucharist speaks to man of his spiritual union with Christ in the heavenlies and declares the goal of his earthly pilgrimage to be union with Christ. It calls on men to "be partakers of the divine nature having escaped the corruption that is in the world through lust" (2 Pet. 1:4). This growth into spiritual maturity through union with Christ is a process of healing whereby man becomes more fully human. In the incarnation God gave us an example of humanity as it was intended to be. In the Eucharist of the church that vision is always held before us.

In the third place *communication is restored in the church through a restored fellowship among people.* Just as sin creates barriers to communication among us, so Christ reconciles us with each other. This reconciliation is experienced within the church. André Bieler put it this way:

> The existence in the midst of society of this cell and nucleus which is the community of Christians, however small it may be, constitutes the small priming for the social restoration of humanness. It is so, of course, if this community is truly Christian. The church community is the society of men and women who through Christ have been restored to their humanness. The church is the embryo of an entirely new world where the once perverted social relations find anew their original nature.[10]

For example, Paul has much to say about the relationship of marriage, comparing the relationship between husband and wife to the one between Christ and the church (see Eph. 5:22–33). He follows this with an admonition for communication between children and parents (see Eph. 6:1–4) and continues to discuss work relationships in Ephesians 6:5–9. The three areas in which society is organized (marriage, family, and work) are restructured in the context of the church. It is interesting that Paul does not see the church as an *additional* society, but as the people of God who function within all the societal roles. The Christian's calling does not appear to be that of a distinct counterculture that runs alongside the larger culture; rather Christians are to be *salt* and *light* in the single society of man in the world. The church, therefore, acts as the renewed society and extends its restored communication and new life throughout the world.

Again, the vision of a new society is seen in the Eucharist. The Eucharist looks back to the death and resurrection of Christ and looks forward to the new heavens and the new earth in which the ultimate messianic banquet will take place. "For as often as you eat this bread and drink this cup, you proclaim the Lord's death till He comes" (1 Cor. 11:26). At the Eucharist the new society is gathered to celebrate the re-creation of man and his world

[10]André Bieler, *The Social Humanism of Calvin* (Richmond: John Knox Press, 1964), pp. 19–20.

through the celebration of the death, resurrection, and second coming of Christ. This new society, now gathered, anticipates the new heavens and the new earth as prophetically imaged in the promise Christ attached to the meaning of the Eucharist.

Fourth, *man's communication with nature is prefigured in the church.* Just as sin broke man's communication with nature so also the work of Christ restores creation to its original intent. Paul wrote of the renewal of creation in Romans:

> . . . the creation itself also will be delivered from the bondage of corruption into the glorious liberty of the children of God. For we know that the whole creation groans and labors with birth pangs together until now. And not only they, but ourselves also who have the firstfruits of the Spirit, even we ourselves groan within ourselves, eagerly waiting for the adoption, the redemption of our body. For we were saved in this hope . . . (Rom. 8:21–24).

The ancient church had a far more in-depth understanding of the restored communication of man with nature than the modern Protestant church has. First, their consciousness was informed by a strong sense of the demonic presence in nature. Paul's insight that "we do not wrestle against flesh and blood, but against principalities, against powers, against the rulers of the darkness of this age, against spiritual wickedness in the heavenly places" (Eph. 6:12) was taken far more seriously than it is taken in the modern scientific world.

The liturgies of ancient Christianity symbolically expressed Christ's victory over the power that evil exercises in nature. The Blessing of Epiphany, for example, proclaims God's power and control over the universe and affirms that man is no longer a slave to evil forces:

> The immaterial powers tremble before thee; the sun praises thee; and the moon worships thee; the stars are thy servants; and light bows to thy will; the tempests tremble and the springs adore thee. Thou didst spread out the heavens like a tent; thou didst set the land upon the waters . . . (therefore) heeding the depth of thy compassion, O Master, thou couldst not bear to see humanity

defeated by the devil, and so thou didst come and didst save us . . .
thou didst free the children of our nature. . . .[11]

When the early church blessed water and sprinkled it on the
land, plants, or houses they were not following some pagan
mystical rite but were acting on a theological insight that nature
had been redeemed. This action of the sanctification of nature is a
proclamation of the renewal of creation through Jesus Christ and,
therefore, of man's communication with it.

The concept of the sanctification of nature is most poignantly
seen in the blessing of the Eucharistic elements. Here bread and
wine have been set aside by the word of prayer to be for God's
people Christ's body and blood. No more dramatic presentation
of the redemption of the natural elements can be made than that.
Thus, in the context of the church and her Eucharist, the proclamation of restored communication with nature is made.

CONCLUSION

It should be valuable at this point to reflect on the content of
this chapter and to ask what the teaching about Christ and His
church has to say to the problem of communication today.

The burden of this chapter has been to stress a single point:
*Christ reversed what Adam did and thus re-created the world.
This new creation is found in the church.*

The implications of this point for communication are as follows:

- There is a place on earth where restored communication is a
  reality—the church. This perspective must be tempered by
  biblical realism, which sees the church in tension between
  what is (the continuing presence of sin) and what will be (the
  fulfillment of the redemption in the consummation.)

- It is the responsibility of the church to achieve and *proclaim*
  the restored communication. In this sense the church must
  be seen as the society that seeks by the Holy Spirit to realize

---

[11]Quoted in Meyendorff, *Byzantine Theology*, p. 135.

the restoration in her practice. The Eucharist always proclaims and holds forth the message of reconciliation.

- The contemporary communicator will best communicate the message of restored communication from the perspective of having experienced it in his life. This places a strong emphasis on the actualization of communication in the church and the experience of it in the Christian community.

III.
IMPLICATIONS FOR CONTEMPORARY COMMUNICATIONS

9
RECOVERING SYMBOLISM

In the preceding chapters my concern has been to concentrate on communication in the context of a biblical view of reality. In this chapter, as well as in the remaining chapters of this work, my concern will be to probe into the future of Christian communication based on the theological understanding already developed. In this chapter and the next we will look at communication *within the church*, and in Chapter 11 we will examine communication *from the church to the world*.

If the church is the restored community, the question is: *How does the church communicate God's reconciliation in her own life?* The concern of this chapter is to focus on symbolism as a medium through which the gospel of reconciliation may be communicated *within* the Christian community.

THE PLACE OF SYMBOLISM

It is generally recognized that a symbol both points beyond itself and participates in that which it symbolizes. For example, Eugene Nida suggests that

> the cross is an iconic symbol of the death of Jesus Christ, for it duplicates in form the instrument by which Jesus was killed, since it has some of the physical characteristics of that event. Similarly, rituals, dramas, pictures, architecture, and dances are iconic in that they "portray" in one way or another some of the physical properties of the referents for which they stand.[1]

---

[1]See Eugene Nida, *Message and Mission* (New York: Harper & Brothers, 1960), p. 65.

The Church as a Symbol

In this sense the church is a symbol of the kingdom. It is not the kingdom itself, but it *points* to the kingdom and *participates* in the kingdom. The church is the presence of the kingdom in the world. The church is the visible expression of the restored creation. It is not a mere ghost-like apparition but a visible, tangible, society of people who have been born into the kingdom and whose new lives are taking shape in the midst of the world. This society of people, bound as they are by time, space, and history, are nevertheless the people of the "new heavens and the new earth." For this reason, the church's life in this world has symbolic significance, both to herself and to the world.

The Significance of Symbols

The fact that the church is a symbol illustrates the significance of symbols. Therefore when we consider the function of symbols as a means of understanding and communicating the Christian faith, we must not treat them as mere psychological creations but as images of *an ultimate reality*. The realm of the supernatural is as real as the natural. Thus, a symbol in the natural world corresponds to a reality of the supernatural world.[2] The church in the world corresponds to the church in the mind of God.

The Necessity of Symbolic Communication

The nature of faith itself demands the transformation of supernatural concepts into visible images and symbols. Because no finite language can fully and completely express supernatural truth adequately, biblical religion and the church in history has always relied on symbolism as a means of communicating that which transcends the realm of the finite. The language of faith has always, therefore, been a language of symbols.[3]

A glance at the history of communications suggests that it has

---

[2]See Everett M. Stowe, *Communicating Reality Through Symbols* (Philadelphia: Westminster Press, 1966).
[3]See Jean Danielou, S.J., *Primitive Christian Symbols* (Baltimore: Helicon Press, 1964); and Gustav Aulén, *The Drama and the Symbols* (Philadelphia: Fortress Press, 1970).

only been recently, and especially within the Protestant Christian community, that symbolic communication has fallen into disuse. The rise of the printed page in the sixteenth century replaced the symbolic form of communication with the written word. The chief form of communication in the West, until the technological developments of the twentieth century, have been reading and writing. The invention of radio, however, signaled a shift toward the recovery of other senses in communication. Sensory communication has accelerated with the introduction of television and new advertising techniques. As man becomes more and more dependent on the visual means of communication, reading and writing skills will go into decline and the impact of the visual will assume greater proportions. This means it is particularly important for the church to once again recapture the use of symbolism as a means of communication. This is especially incumbent upon Protestants, whose reform was sparked and spread by the revolution introduced by the Gutenberg press.

IMPLICATIONS FOR COMMUNICATION WITHIN THE CHURCH

The obvious implication of symbolism as a means of communicating the Christian message is *the need to recover the use of symbolism in the church*. There are several reasons why Christians (I refer particularly to Protestant-evangelicals) need to recover symbolic expression.

First, there has been a *loss of the use of symbolism among Protestants*. As Christians we are accustomed to simple and straightforward language. The use of imagery, symbols, and even subtle language is relatively unknown among many Protestants who thoughtlessly have locked themselves into discursive expression as the preferable, if not the only, form of communication.

One reason why we evangelicals prefer verbal communication has to do with our view of the Bible. We see the Bible as a Book of words. It is God's *written* revelation. This emphasis on the written words of Scripture coupled with an attitude of neglect toward the symbolic forms of communication (which constitute a large

portion of Scripture) cause a loss of understanding—and blessing.

Another reason we are stuck with words as the major means of
communication is found in our strong sense of man as a *reasonable* creature. Today a strong emphasis is placed on the mind of
man. Because man above all other creatures is rational, he is able
to investigate the words of Scripture and derive from them the
correct meaning of things. Therefore, the emphasis falls on *words*
and *cognitive understanding* in communication.

While words and objectified understanding play an important
part in communication and should not be denied, there is
nevertheless another dimension of communication that needs
further exploration—symbolism. Symbolic communication is affirmed in the Scriptures. Scripture is filled with visions, dreams,
imagery and apocalyptic material as previously discussed.
Furthermore, the assumption that man is predominantly a *verbal*
creature greatly underestimates the emotive side of man.

A second reason to recover symbolism is found in the recognition that *man is a symbolic creature.* For example, recent
research in psychology, especially that branch which attempts to
understand the neural organization of man's mind, has concluded
that man's brain functions differently in the right and left
hemispheres. The left hemisphere appears to specialize in verbal
functions, and the right hemisphere centers on spatial functions
and other nonverbal skills.

This is the concern of Stephen G. Meyer in an article entitled
"Neuropsychology and Worship." He sets out to relate the find-
ings of neural investigation to the experience of worship.[4] His
argument, which begins with Scripture, is that (1) while Scripture is verbal, the material it communicates is based on a variety
of communication models, ranging from discursive expression to
highly apocalyptic language to poetic discourse; (2) although
Christianity is grounded on reason, illustrated by Paul's reasoning from the Scriptures in the synagogue (see Acts 17:2) or
Peter's insisting that Christians give "a defense to everyone who

[4]See Stephen G. Meyer, "Neuropsychology and Worship," *Journal of Psychology and
Theology* (Fall, 1975), pp. 281–89.

asks you a reason for the hope that is in you . . ." (1 Pet. 3:15), there are nevertheless "definitive confrontations between God and man where there is concurrent use of vision and word."[5] Meyer cites the examples of Ezekiel, Job, and John (Revelation) and concludes "while the Bible presents the Christian faith as a rational faith, the rationale is built on symbols which outline its structure."[6]

Rollo May argues that the loss of symbols constitutes one of man's chief difficulties. Because man has no symbols to identify and illustrate the meaning of life, he cannot transcend the crises of his life. Hunger, war, death, unemployment, disease, and the other horrors that confront man on a daily basis seem to be the sum and substance of life. Without signs or symbols in *this world* to show man another world or a means of coping with the trials and strains of this world, man has nowhere to turn but to despair and absurdity.[7]

A third reason to recover symbolism is rooted in the recognition that *symbolism is at the very center of life itself.* The celebrations of birthdays, anniversaries, graduations, marriages, funerals, and the like are all ways of *acting out* the meaning of things that words alone fail to convey.

Likewise, the great drama of the world as expressed in Scripture, from the fall of man to the restoration of man (and his world) in Jesus Christ, ought to be communicated not only in words but in the actions of the church. Symbolic communication in the church is a valid means of communicating truths of the Christian faith. The reenactment of the birth of Christ, the sorrow over His death, the joy of His resurrection, and the power of Pentecost cannot be completely nor adequately communicated through words alone. If man is a creature whose brain is oriented toward spatial as well as verbal communication, then *Christian communication, both within the church and outside the church, must not neglect the symbolic, nonverbal, and ritualistic means of communication.*

[5] Ibid., p. 285.
[6] Ibid., p. 286.
[7] Rollo May, "The Healing Power of Symbols," *Pastoral Psychology* (Nov., 1960), pp. 37–49.

WAYS TO RECOVER SYMBOLISM

It is my intention to set forth some specific examples through which a symbolic communication of the Christian message can be made. This is a broad subject and deserves a book in itself. I will limit myself, therefore, to symbolic communication through worship.[8]

The Symbolic Nature of Christian Worship

What is worship? The English word for worship comes from the word *worth* and means to ascribe worth to God. In Isaiah 6 and again in Revelation 4, the creatures of God are ascribing worth to God for who He is. Both Isaiah and John were smitten with the holiness of God and heard the creatures who surrounded the throne cry "Holy, holy, holy,/Lord God Almighty,/Who was and is and is to come!" (Rev. 4:8, cf. Isa. 6:3).

A fascinating feature about this vision is the symbolism that surrounded God on His throne. Isaiah saw Him "sitting on a throne, lofty and exalted, with the train of His robe filling the temple. Seraphim stood above Him, each having six wings; with two he covered his face, and with two he covered his feet, and with two he flew" (Isa. 6:1,2). John's description is more elaborate:

> He who sat there was like jasper and a sardius stone in appearance; and there was a rainbow around the throne, in appearance like an emerald. And around the throne were twenty-four thrones, and on the thrones I saw twenty-four elders sitting, clothed in white robes; and they had crowns of gold on their heads. And out of the throne proceeded lightnings, thunderings, and voices. And there were seven lamps of fire burning before the throne, which are the seven Spirits of God. And before the throne there was a sea of glass, like crystal . . . (Rev. 4:3–6).

The important features of these visions (which affected the

---

[8]The liturgical renewal of the last two decades has produced numerous works of worship. One of the latest works, which combines previous scholarship and contains a complete bibliography, is Cheslyn Jones, Geoffrey Wainwright, and Edward Yarnold, S.J., eds., *The Study of Liturgy* (New York: Oxford University Press, 1978).

early development of Christian worship) are the visual images that speak to the greatness and the ultimate nature of God. All creatures of God, including creation itself, fall before Him to ascribe power and glory to Him because of who He is.

The Loss of Symbolism in Worship

It is quite evident that the symbolic vision of worship has been lost in many churches. A reason for this lies in the lack of balance within the church's self-understanding.

The church has always understood herself in terms of the following dimensions: a worshiping community; a learning community; a mission community; a fellowship community; a healing community; a servant community. Unfortunately a balance of all these aspects of the church is rarely achieved. A church may emphasize worship but not evangelism; teaching but not service; evangelism but not worship.

In the case of Protestant evangelicals the tendency is to emphasize evangelism (mission) and teaching (learning) to the neglect of the other aspects, particularly worship. For that reason I have chosen to illustrate how the gospel may be communicated symbolically through worship. I do not advocate less emphasis on evangelism and teaching. I am simply calling for balance through the recovery of worship.

Recovering Symbolism in Worship

If worship means to ascribe worth to God, then we need to ask *how* we should worship. In both the Old and New Testaments three reasons are given why God's people should ascribe worth to Him. They are (1) because He created all things (see Exod. 20:11 and Rev. 4:11); (2) because He has redeemed a people for Himself (see Deut. 5:15 and Rev. 5:9); and (3) because He has entered into covenant community with His people (see Exod. 24:3–8 and Rev. 5:10).

The designation of the people of God in both the Old Testament (*Q'hal*) and the New Testament (*Ecclesia*) has as its root meaning *the people who are gathered for worship.*

The public worship of the church is therefore a corporate act in which the church as the covenant community rehearses both who

God is and what God has done. In this way the church ascribes worth to God and gives glory to His name. Worship is essentially directed toward God (although it includes God's speaking to us through His Word by the Holy Spirit). We do not go to church to get something for ourselves. Rather the community gathers together to give ascriptions of praise and worth to God.

This element of Christian experience is missing whenever the church regards public worship as the time to evangelize or the time to teach. We no longer have a time to worship.

The problem of discussing worship as symbolic is compounded by the problem of not setting a time aside for worship. Let us assume, however, that church renewal has the effect of restoring worship within the Protestant evangelical community. What principles should guide the restoration of symbolism in our worship? I will mention four.

First, it will be necessary to recognize that *earthly worship is modeled after a heavenly pattern.* The visions of Isaiah and John affirm and do not negate the use of symbolism in worship. Obviously it is impossible and not advisable to literally reproduce the elements of their visions. On the other hand, a refusal to incorporate visual symbols in worship is a resistance by the earthly church to join the heavenly hosts in ascribing worth to God. But how may the church on earth enter into visual, symbolic worship? A church building itself may represent the heavenlies while the chancel represents the throne of God. In this context the ministers, the choir, and the congregation envision themselves as the servants of God who gather around His throne to proclaim His worth. The aesthetic setting in which this takes place could range all the way from a Byzantine cathedral to a simple chapel. The thing of ultimate importance is not the gold and glitter, but the triggering of the worshipers' imaginations and spirits through the visual and symbolic setting.

Second, it is important for us to *recover worship as an action.* It is something we do . . . not something that is done to us. The visions given in Isaiah and Revelation indicate that worshipers are not merely passive observers. They were involved in *doing* something. In the account of John, the creatures "do not rest day or night," the elders "fall down before Him," and "cast their crowns before the throne" (Rev. 4:8,10). Worship involves an active response of the worshiper.

In the history of Christian worship there has been a strong emphasis on what the worshiper does. In the Catholic and Orthodox traditions the worshiper genuflects, kneels, sings numerous responses, bows, says "amen" at the end of the prayers, walks forward for Communion, smells the incense, hears the bells, sees the Host, and passes the kiss of peace. Charismatic worship is also quite active. Charismatics raise their hands, speak in tongues, interpret, prophesy, sing in the Spirit, and sometimes dance spontaneously. In this sense the Catholics, the Orthodox, the Charismatics, and others who stress the involvement of the whole person in worship are using a greater variety of communication means than those who merely sit and expect to be challenged or filled.

Third, *we cannot neglect time, space, and history as elements of worship.* There is a timeless character to the worship described by Isaiah and John. Although worship takes place in time, space, and history, the church recognizes that these elements have an eternal character. For example, time has always been interpreted in relationship to the coming of Christ, to His life and ministry, to His death and resurrection, to the coming of the Holy Spirit in the life of the church, and to the second coming of Christ. These events, all of which are *historical*, are gathered up into the liturgy of the church and reenacted symbolically.

Because space also belongs to the Lord by virtue of creation and redemption, the redeemed nature of space may be demonstrated in the architectural arrangement of the building (both inside and outside). These forms of communication played an important part in the witness of the ancient church. A study of the development of the church year, of the feasts and festivals that celebrated the great drama of the birth, the death, the resurrection, and the coming of the Holy Spirit, as well as an examination of the redemptive understanding of art and architecture need to be revived in this age of the return to the visual.

Fourth, we must always keep in mind that *worship is a learned art.* The idea that worship is instantaneous, spontaneous, and natural betrays man's self-understanding in practically every area of life. We are more than willing to agree that a successful musician, artist, dramatist, salesman, doctor, teacher, lawyer, carpenter, or housewife must *learn* the art of doing his or her profession right! Yet when it comes to the Christian faith, to worship, and to the communication of Christian truths, we somehow feel that it should all fall into place naturally without any effort on our part. For this reason it is important to emphasize both the *learned* and *artistic* nature of worship. The process by which it has been learned is historical.

In order to help you the reader understand more of what I am saying I will illustrate the symbolic dimension of worship as practiced in the early church. My examples are drawn from the sacraments of Baptism, Chrismation and the Eucharist. I do not intend to argue that Protestant evangelicals should adopt a slavish adherence to the symbolism used in the early church. Rather, I intend to provide illustrations that will enrich the understanding of what we already do and encourage the development of the increased use of symbolism.

BAPTISM, CHRISMATION, AND THE EUCHARIST

The Symbolic Nature of Baptism

The church needs to take a closer look at symbols as a means of communicating God's truth through such acts of worship as ordination of ministers and elders, consecration of bishops, marriages, funerals, confirmations or dedications, and holy baptism. Because space will not permit the treatment of all of these occasions, I will draw from *The Apostolic Tradition* written by Hippolytus in A.D. 220.[9] His writing gives us special insight into the forms of worship used in antiquity and, especially for our purposes, knowledge of the symbolic elements through which the gospel message was communicated in Baptism, Chrismation and the Eucharist. My approach will be to put the writing of Hippolytus in the left column and comment on the use of symbolism in the right column.

---

[9]Hippolytus, *The Apostolic Tradition*, ed. Burton Scott Eaton (Harnden, Conn.: Archon Books, 1962), pp. 44--9.

I. Preparation

They who are to be set apart for baptism shall be chosen after their lives have been examined: whether they have visited the sick, whether they have been active in well-doing. When their sponsors have testified that they have done these things, then let them hear the Gospel. Then from the time that they are separated from other catechumens, hands shall be laid upon them daily in exorcism and, as the day of their baptism draws near, the bishop himself shall exorcise each one of them that he may be personally assured of their purity. Then, if there is any of them who is not good or pure, he shall be put aside as not having heard the word in faith; for it is never possible for the alien to be concealed.

Then those who are set apart for baptism shall be instructed to bathe and free themselves from impurity and wash themselves on Thursday. If a woman is menstruous, she shall be set aside and baptized on some other day.

They who are to be baptized shall fast on Friday, and on Saturday the bishop shall as-

Preparation for Christian baptism contained many symbols such as:

Examination: For three years candidates were instructed in orthodoxy (correct doctrine) and orthoproxy (correct living). As the time of baptism drew near, they were reviewed as to their growth in Christian living: Has the grace of God *taken hold?* Only those who were of good report were set aside for baptism.

Being Set Aside: During six weeks before baptism candidates went through an intense period of personal preparation (Most scholars see this as the origin of Lent. Gradually the whole church joined the candidates in special preparation for Easter.) Normally in the early church, baptism occurred only once a year—on Easter, a further strengthening of the symbolic union with Christ.

Fasting: a symbol of repentance derived from the Old Testament, practiced in the New, and continued by the early church. Abstinence from food helps a person concentrate on repentance and spiritual preparation for baptism.

semble them and command them to kneel in prayer. And, laying his hand upon them, he shall exorcise all evil spirits to flee away and never to return; when he has done this he shall breathe in their faces, seal their foreheads, ears and noses, and then raise them up. They shall spend all that night in vigil, listening to reading and instruction.

They who are to be baptized shall bring with them no other vessels than the one each will bring for the eucharist; for it is fitting that he who is counted worthy of baptism should bring his offering at that time.

Exorcism: a symbolic expression of the power of Christ over evil. Because Christ conquered and destroyed the evil one, prayer in the name of Christ is a demonstration of the power of Christ to deliver that person from evil. It is also used over water as a sign of God's power to deliver nature from the effect of sin.

Water: a strikingly rich biblical symbol. It represents creative power both for evil and good. By water, God created the world. In water our first birth occurs. In New Testament times it was believed that demonic powers were in the sea. In water, then, Christ's power over Satan is dramatically portrayed. Combining water as an expression of God's creative power with Christ's authority over the demonic in water makes it a powerful symbol of new life.

Breath: a symbol of the Spirit. God breathed into man "the breath of life; and man became a living being" (Gen. 2:7). Man lost the Spirit at the fall which is regained at salvation. The breath symbolically represents the return of God's Spirit to man, making him whole again.

Seal: The seal or imprint of God was made on the person by the sign of the cross. The seal indicated that this person belonged to God and that his total person (all the senses) belonged to the service of God.

II. The Baptism

At cockcrow prayer shall be made over the water. The stream shall flow through the baptismal tank or pour into it from above when there is no scarcity of water; but if there is a scarcity, whether constant or sudden, then use whatever water you can find.

They shall remove their clothing. And first baptize the little ones; if they can speak for themselves, they shall do so; if not, their parents or other relatives shall speak for them. Then baptize the men, and last of all the women; they must first loosen their hair and put aside any gold or silver ornaments that they were wearing: let no one take any alien thing down to the water with them.

At the hour set for the baptism the bishop shall give thanks over oil and put it into a vessel: this is called the "oil of thanksgiving." And he shall take other oil and exorcise it: this is called "the oil of exor-

Removal of clothing: This action represented "putting off" the old man.

Oil of thanksgiving and oil of exorcism: Both these oils represented putting off the old and putting on the new. The oil of exorcism was used in the prayer of renunciation and the oil of thanksgiving was used in the prayer for the reception of the Holy Spirit.

Renunciation: Facing the west (which symbolically represented the seat of Satan), the candidate renounced the power of evil in his life.

Confession and triune immersions: The candidate was baptized three times to represent a triune faith. Immersion represented an identification with Father, Son, and Holy Spirit. The confession was a symbol of what the candidate believed.

Clothed: The candidate was clothed with a white new garment to signify "putting on"

cism." (The anointing is performed by a presbyter.) A deacon shall bring the oil of exorcism, and shall stand at the presbyter's left hand; and another deacon shall take the oil of thanksgiving, and shall stand at the presbyter's right hand. Then the presbyter, taking hold of each of those about to be baptized, shall command him to renounce, saying:

> I renounce thee,
> Satan, and all thy
> servants and all
> thy works.

And when he has renounced all these, the presbyter shall anoint him with the oil of exorcism, saying:

> Let all spirits
> depart far from
> thee.

Then, after these things, let him give him over to the presbyter who baptizes, and let the candidates stand in the water, naked, a deacon going with them likewise. And when he who is being baptized goes down into the water, he who baptizes him, putting his hand on him, shall say thus:

> Dost thou believe
> in God, the Father
> Almighty?

Jesus Christ. It is thought by some that the description of Revelation 6:9 is similar to the scene of the white-robed, newly baptized Christians.

Brought into the church: The baptismal font in many churches was located by the entrance, symbolizing entrance into the church through baptism into Jesus Christ. The walk into the church was a symbolic entrance into the body of Christ.

THE APOSTOLIC TRADITION   *EXPLANATION*

And he who is being baptized
shall say:

I believe.

Then holding his hand placed on
his head, he shall baptize him
once. And then he shall say:

Dost thou believe
in Christ Jesus, the
Son of God, who was
born of the Holy Ghost
of the Virgin Mary,
and was crucified
under Pontius Pilate,
and was dead and
buried, and rose
again the third day,
alive from the dead,
and ascended into
heaven, and sat at
the right hand of the
Father, and will come
to judge the quick and
the dead?

And when he says,

I believe,

he is baptized again. And again
he shall say,

Dost thou believe in the
Holy Ghost, and the
holy church, and the
resurrection of the
flesh?

He who is being baptized shall
say accordingly:

I believe,

and so he is baptized a third time.

And afterward, when he has come up (out of the water), he is anointed by the presbyter with the oil of thanksgiving, the presbyter saying:

> I anoint thee with
> holy oil in the name
> of Jesus Christ.

And so each one, after drying himself, is immediately clothed, and then is brought into the church.

III. Chrismation

Then the bishop, laying his hand upon them, shall pray, saying:

> O Lord God, who
> hast made them
> worthy to obtain
> remission of sins
> through the laver
> of regeneration of
> the Holy Spirit,
> send into them thy
> grace, that they
> may serve thee
> according to thy
> will; for thine is
> the glory, to the
> Father and the Son,
> with the Holy Spirit
> in the holy church,
> both now and world
> without end. Amen.

Laying on of hands: A New Testament custom (taken from the Old Testament) that symbolizes the reception of the Holy Spirit. This action occurred in conjunction with the washing in the oil of thanksgiving.

Prayer: A symbol of unity with the people of God and with God.

Kiss of peace: A symbol of reconciliation both toward God and with fellow believers that occurred before the Eucharist.

Then, pouring the oil of thanksgiving from his hand and putting it on his forehead, he shall say:

> I anoint thee with
> holy oil in the Lord,
> the Father Almighty
> and Christ Jesus and
> the Holy Ghost.

And signing them on the forehead he shall say:

> The Lord be with
> thee;

and he who is signed shall say:

> And with thy spirit.

And so he shall do to each one.

And immediately thereafter they shall join in prayer with all the people, but they shall not pray with the faithful until all these things are completed. And at the close of their prayer they give the kiss of peace.

IV. Eucharist

And then the offering is immediately brought by the deacons to the bishop, and by thanksgiving he shall make the bread into an image of the body of Christ, and the cup of wine mixed with water according to the likeness of the blood, which is shed for all who believe in

Water and wine: Symbols of the cross. Christ poured forth both blood and water from His body.

Milk and honey: Symbols of the future promised to Israel, of which the Christian now receives.

him. And milk and honey mixed together for the fulfillment of the promise to the fathers, which spoke of a land flowing with milk and honey; namely, Christ's flesh which he gave, by which they who believe are nourished like babes, he making sweet the bitter things of the heart by the gentleness of his word. And the water into an offering in a token of the laver, in order that the inner part of man, which is a living soul, may receive the same as the body.

Breaks the bread: Symbol of the body broken for man.

Distributes: Symbol of Christ who gave Himself.

Good works: The continuing symbol of the presence of Christ in the life of the believer. Christ, who is met and received in the Eucharist, is lived out in the life of the believer and thereby continues to be communicated.

The bishop shall explain the reason of all these things to those who partake. And when he breaks the bread and distributes the fragments he shall say:

> The heavenly bread
> in Christ Jesus.

And the recipient shall say, Amen.

And the presbyters—or if there are not enough presbyters, the deacons—shall hold the cups, and shall stand by with reverence and modesty; first he who holds the water, then the milk, thirdly the wine. And the recipients shall taste of each three times, he who gives the cup saying:

> In God the Father
> Almighty;

and the recipient shall say, Amen. Then:

In the Holy Ghost
and the holy church;

and he shall say, Amen. So it shall be done to each.

And when these things are completed, let each one hasten to do good works, and to please God and to live aright, devoting himself to the church, practising the things he has learned, advancing in the service of God.

Now we have briefly delivered to you these things concerning the holy baptism and the holy oblation, for you have already been instructed concerning the resurrection of the flesh and all other things as taught in Scripture. Yet if there is any other thing that ought to be told (to converts), let the bishop impart it to them privately after their baptism; let not unbelievers know it, until they are baptized: this is the white stone of which John said: "There is upon it a new name written, which no one knoweth but he that receiveth the stone."

Implications

This brief examination of *The Apostolic Tradition* shows the significance of symbolic communication in the early church. Through symbols the whole gospel of man's reconciliation with

God, with himself, with fellow man, and with nature was communicated.

This example makes it clear that we are not limited to words as the only means of communication. But what does this fact imply for worship today?

In the first place *the Christian view of creation, redemption, and covenant community can be expressed through the art of recitation.* The ancient liturgy of the church, drawing from the synagogue, has placed a high priority on the Word read and spoken. This is, of course, a verbal emphasis. Recitation, however, properly understood is an art. Recitation intends to recreate. It is not a mere "dead" reading or preaching. We ought to do much more in our churches to improve the ability of communication through reading the Scripture and preaching. We need to learn how to proclaim through recitation.

A proclamation is more like an announcement than a treatise and should be delivered with a sense of urgency, clarity, and precision. Thus scriptural proclamation ought to be characterized by dynamic power and not be a mere statement of fact. It is a lively Word, one that "shall not return to Me empty,/Without accomplishing what I desire,/And without succeeding in the matter for which I sent it" (Isa. 55:11). Much liturgical reading of the Word is characterized by dullness; and too much of our preaching sounds like a moral diatribe or an outdated lecture. Reading and preaching, properly executed, can trigger the imagination and create visual images, thus communicating the reality it presents.[10]

In the second place *we must recover that sense in which the truth of the Christian message may be expressed through the art of rehearsal.* Rehearsal is the dramatic re-creation of a significant event through which God has revealed Himself savingly. In worship we rehearse and re-present the great events of redemptive history.

The origin for dramatic re-presentation in worship lies in the

[10]See Clyde H. Ried, "Preaching and the Nature of Communications," *Pastoral Psychology* (Oct. 1963), pp. 40-9.

Old Testament experience. Catholic theologian Monika Hellwig comments,

> The characteristic genius of Israel manifests itself in the festal celebration of Pesach or Passover, where the event is ritually rehearsed so that the present generation may enter into it, become a part of it, assimilate its meaning, and be transformed by it. Across the barriers of space and time, in the Passover Seder all Israel becomes part of the event of the great liberation of the Exodus, and in that event comes into communion with God who acts in history.[11]

Even as the Passover is the rehearsal of a past event, which by its reenactment makes it a present reality for the worshiper, so the Christian Eucharist rehearses the central event of the Christian message and proclaims the saving work of Christ through dramatic re-presentation.

In this Word dramatized, the Christian church has always recognized the central action of worship whereby the mystery of God incarnate is presented visibly. In this action, through the symbols of bread and wine, the words of institution, the prayer of consecration, and the giving and receiving of the elements, a real communication takes place. Here the God of history is made present in a visible and tangible way, proclaiming His saving work through the senses of sight, touch, smell, and taste.

All the aspects of restoration are realized in this action: Man communes with God; man communes with himself in recognizing that his sins are forgiven; he communes with his neighbor in the community of reconciled believers; he communes with nature by receiving the blessed bread and wine, which proclaim the reconciliation of all things to God through Jesus Christ. Furthermore, the Eucharist points to the future for it proclaims the death of Christ "till He comes." It lifts man out of the mundane and speaks to him of the ultimate meaning of life, that this world is not all that

---

[11]Monika K. Hellwig, "Christian Eucharist in Relation to Jewish Worship," *The Journal of Ecumenical Studies* (Spring, 1976), p. 325.

is, that his ultimate destiny is in the new heavens and the new earth.

By the same token, the Eucharistic symbols do *not* deny the reality of this world. Rather, by bringing the past and the future together, the Eucharist communicates the meaning of history and of man's place in it. It therefore properly sends man forth into the world to be a continuing agent of God's reconciliation to the world. This is the hope that has been expressed in the symbol of the redeemed community, the church, especially in her worship.

CONCLUSION

We have cited only a *few* examples of symbolic communication from the history of the church. The interested reader will want to examine various church liturgies for special holy days such as Christmas, Easter, and Pentecost. Symbolism can be seen also in the vestments, architecture, and music of the church. Each of these areas will provide ideas for recovering symbolism in the contemporary church.[12]

But what of the future? How are we to view the changes occurring in communications in the twentieth century? How should these changes affect our approach to symbolic communication? A single point will suffice: *The communication of the Christian message must be directed toward the emotive as well as the cognitive level of man.* This is a legitimate field into which the church may enter. Involvement in visual communication techniques has both biblical and theological support.[13]

In this chapter I have focused on symbolism as a medium through which the gospel of our reconciliation may be communicated *within* the Christian community.

Here is a summary of the major points I have made:

- The church is the earthly symbol of the kingdom. A symbol

[12] I refer the reader to the bibliographies in each of these areas contained in *The Study of Liturgy* (see footnote 8).
[13] An example of future probing is found in Edward N. McNulty, *Gadgets, Gimmicks and Grace: A Handbook on Multi-Media in Church and School* (St. Meinard, Ind.: Abbey Press, 1976).

participates in the reality it presents. Therefore, in the church we may expect to find an expression of restored relationships.

- The new relationships between man and God, man and himself, man and his fellowman, and man and nature are proclaimed in the symbolism of worship.

- Therefore, the church today, if she would communicate the reality of new life in Christ, must recover symbolism in which the truth of Christian reconciliation is not only heard, but also experienced with the senses of touch, taste, smell, and sight.

10
RECOVERING NURTURE

The concern of this chapter is how growth in Christ is communicated in the church. Because the church finds herself between Pentecost and the consummation she is still in the state of the *now* and the *not yet*. She has been redeemed, but her redemption is not yet complete. Her calling, therefore, in the world is to *grow in Christ*. This is true both for individual members and for the church corporate. The church is, as Paul said, "built on the foundation of the apostles and prophets, Jesus Christ Himself being the chief cornerstone, in whom the whole building, being joined together, *grows* into a holy Temple in the Lord" (Eph. 2:20,21).

WHAT IS GROWTH?

It is generally recognized that spiritual growth is the transformation of the person in at least the following four areas: knowledge, attitudes, behavior, and skills.[1]

Knowledge

The church has always concerned herself with the communication of *knowledge*, and this is because Christianity is a message with content. Christians have modeled themselves after Paul in Thessalonica where he "reasoned with them from the Scriptures, explaining and demonstrating that the Christ had to suffer and rise again from the dead . . ." (Acts 17:2,3).

One problem the church has faced, especially among those of a

---

[1] For development of these areas, see Benjamin Franklin Jackson, ed., *Communication: Learning for Churchmen* (Nashville: Abingdon Press, 1968).

rationalistic bent, is to stress growth only as the accumulation of knowledge. The emphasis among these church leaders is on the memorization of facts, the storing of objective data. The problem in this approach is not so much the gaining of knowledge, but the gaining of knowledge *without interpretation*. Knowledge that leads to understanding, wisdom, and action should be the goal of the church. It is the kind of knowledge that leads to growth.

Attitude

An attitude may be described as a mental position in relation to a frame of reference. Since the Christian view of reality is a frame of reference, we may refer to a Christian attitude as the stance of a person toward life in general.

Paul, for example, set forth an attitude in Romans 8:28 when he said, ". . . we know that all things work together for good to those who love God, to those who are the called according to His purpose."

Peter as well was developing a Christian attitude in his readers who were suffering under the persecution by Nero. He exhorted, "Do not think it strange concerning the fiery trial which is to try you, as though some strange thing happened to you; but rejoice insofar as you are partakers of Christ's sufferings, that when His glory is revealed you may also be glad with exceeding joy" (1 Pet. 4:12,13).

The attitudes communicated here by Paul and Peter are both Christian because they are biblical *and* universal. The problem, however, in the church today is that we too often overlook the communication of a truly Christian and universal attitude, replacing it with a parochial or subcultural *ethos*.

For example, in America the attitudes of capitalism, individualism, and success are often mistakenly identified with the Christian faith. Or, we capitulate to the "I'm right, you're wrong" syndrome and divide ourselves from other Christians on matters of secondary importance, creating attitudes of superiority, prejudice, divisiveness, and arrogance. No one can be part of the church very long without coming up against these wrong attitudes. What we desire is the communication of attitudes and perspectives on life that are truly Christian, not subcultural.

Behavior

Growth also occurs in the area of behavior.[2] The Christian emphasis, like the Old Testament, places a high priority on life-style.

The new community is distinguished by its willingness to put on a new habit of life. Paul spoke of Christians as those who once "presented your members as servants to uncleanness, and to lawlessness leading to more lawlessness" but now as those who "present your members as servants to righteousness for holiness" (Rom. 6:19). They are those who "walk in the Spirit" and not in the "lust of the flesh" (Gal. 5:16; see also vv. 17–26). They put off the old and put on the new (see Col. 3:1–17).

A problem that has plagued the church in the past and continues to be a problem today, is the tendency to address behavior only from a moralistic perspective, while forgetting to inform people of the power of the Holy Spirit.

We instruct our children to do good or be good, telling them that is what God wants of them. In this way we make the Christian faith into a burdensome list of do's and don'ts. Instead, we ought to emphasize the freedom and power and righteousness we have in Christ to become the persons we were born the second time to be. This emphasis sets us free from legalism and places the accent on growth in Christ through the power of the Holy Spirit.

Moralism by itself may also be a deceptive twisting of Scripture for the purpose of communicating one's preferred behavioral standards. This method, which often overly moralizes Scripture, misses the redemptive meaning of Scripture and fails to see the hope of a new creation. It replaces the underlying structure of redemption with moralistic lessons and "do-goodisms." While moral living may be communicated, the end product is based on a shallow and superficial perception of things rather than on the more deeply biblical view of the newly created order in which the values of the kingdom are lived out. In the end, therefore,

---

[2]See David Hesselgrave, *Communicating Christ Cross-Culturally* (Grand Rapids: Zondervan, 1978), chs. 30, 31.

moralism itself is unable to produce the growth and stability it seeks to inculcate.

Skills

Finally, the church is concerned to communicate skills.[3] Jesus said, "You will receive power when the Holy Spirit has come upon you; and you will be witnesses to Me in Jerusalem, and in all Judea and Samaria, and to the end of the earth" (Acts 1:8).

The church has the responsibility not only to witness but also to function as a body, each member exercising his or her own gifts within the community. Paul wrote of "diversities of activities" (1 Cor. 12:6). In the same context Paul said the skills given to each person have to do with "mutual profit." Not everyone has the same skill, but each one with his skill contributes to the continued growth of the entire body.

A problem in the church today is that we expect the minister to have all the skills for Christian ministry while the congregation looks on. The discovery and implementation of skills (whether teaching, preaching, counseling, administration, helping the needy, ministering to the sick or the dying, caring for the widows and orphans) must become a priority if the church is to survive in secular society.

Having looked at growth in knowledge, attitudes, behavior, and skills, we must now turn to our second question: How does growth occur? This question is best answered by those who recognize *the church as a living community of people, the household of God. The church is the context in which growth occurs. It is the family of God and as such nurtures and trains its members who have been born into it.*

THE CHURCH AS THE CONTEXT FOR GROWTH

The Holy Spirit Works Through the Church

We have already seen that the mystery of communication is

[3]See Ray C. Stedman, *Body Life* (Glendale, Calif.: L/C Regal Books, 1973).

rooted in understanding the triune God. God has made Himself present to us in history as the Father, as the incarnate Son, and as the Holy Spirit in the life of the church. The community of fellowship within the Godhead is not only made known to us but draws us into the triune experience of fellowship.

In Christian theology we do not think of the community of the Godhead as a mere model. It is not something we are called to emulate, as much as we are called to *participate* in it. Think of it! God who is utterly complete in Himself, perfectly happy in the community and fellowship of Father, Son, and Holy Spirit not only creates but offers His creation a relationship in the community of the Godhead.

The Israelites gradually came to see that the covenant they entered into with God (see Exod. 19–24) was a relationship that offered them great familiarity with Him. He was the God of creation and battles, but He also spoke of Himself as Israel's father, as a Husband who had taken Israel to Himself in an unending love. In spite of Israel's infidelities through the centuries, God continued to love and care for His people.

The Israelites recognized God's nearness to them and perceived His "dwelling" with them. He appeared to them at Mount Sinai; He was present in the ark and made His abode in the Holy of Holies. In the New Testament, God's nearness took on a new quality in His personalization in Jesus Christ. In Christ, the Godhead actually became a Person and lived in the community of man as part of that fellowship. In Christ, as we have seen, a new creation began. The church is the expression of that new life, and to the church Christ promised the gift of the Holy Spirit.

In John 14, Jesus told His disciples He was to go away but that He would not leave them desolate, promising to send the Holy Spirit: "But the Helper, the Holy Spirit, whom the Father will send in My name, He will teach you all things, and bring to your remembrance all things that I have said to you" (John 14:26).

The Mission of the Spirit

In the above verse we were introduced to the *mission* of the Spirit. By sending the Spirit to those who believe in Him, Christ desires to share with us the unity He has with the Father. Thus, through faith we are united with the Father, the Son, and the Holy Spirit; we enter into the communion of the Godhead! This communal relationship was accomplished at Pentecost and recognized by Peter as a fulfillment of the Old Testament prophecy of Joel: *"Thus you will know that I am in the midst of Israel,/*And that I am the LORD your God/And there is no other . . ."* (Joel 2:27, italics mine; see also vv. 28,29 and Acts 2:17–21).

It is in the church, the mystical body of Christ, that the Holy Spirit dwells. He enters into organic union with each Christian as the "temple" of the Holy Spirit (". . . your body is the temple of the Holy Spirit who is in you, whom you have from God . . ." 1 Cor. 6:19). Because of this indwelling, the church as a whole becomes the temple of the Holy Spirit ("in whom the whole building, being joined together, grows into a holy temple in the Lord in whom you also are being built together for a habitation of God in the Spirit" Eph. 2:21,22).

The Holy Spirit Enlivens Our Union With Christ

It is in the context of the *church* then, which is in inseparable union with the Godhead, that spiritual growth is to take place. Spiritual growth is not merely accumulating knowledge or adopting a moralistic set of rules; *it is the process of becoming adept at communing with God the Father through Jesus Christ by the Holy Spirit.*

It is the special role of the Holy Spirit to enable our growth. Whereas our Lord Jesus Christ is the *mediator* between God and man, the Holy Spirit is the *communicator* between God and man. He communicates God to man and man to God as Paul stated: "Because you are sons, God has sent forth the Spirit of His Son into your hearts, crying out, *'Abba!* Father!' Therefore you are no longer a servant but a son, and if a son, then an heir of God through Christ" (Gal. 4:6,7). This passage speaks to us of the *power* of the Spirit who works in the very heart of the Christian, transforming him into the image of Christ (see Rom. 12:2).

Specifically, the work of the Holy Spirit is to communicate *within us* a transforming power that will reshape our whole lives. It is not just a matter of thinking differently (it is that too), but a matter of living differently. The Bible makes it very clear that we are not to exhibit works of the flesh (see Gal. 5:19–21) but fruit of the Spirit. This fruit is a description of a lifestyle. It presupposes that "those who are Christ's have crucified the flesh with its passions and desires" (Gal. 5:24) and have chosen to display "love, joy, peace, longsuffering, kindness, goodness, faithfulness, gentleness, self-control" (Gal. 5:22,23). In this respect the Holy Spirit's function is to mold both within and without the life of the believer who is growing into union with God. The historical and social context in which this occurs is in the church, which, by the providence of God, has been called to be the new community in a world of broken relationships.

The Church as the Nurturing Community

The church is a nurturing community because in and through the church, as the body of Christ, the Holy Spirit works to mold the character of each member so that a growth in Christ is occurring, a maturation is communicated.[4]

In general, the whole life of the church may be viewed from the standpoint of nurture: It is modeled in the church's historical heritage, in her social context, and in her vision of the future.

First of all, *nurture is modeled through the historical heritage of the church.* By this notion I especially refer to the way in which the Holy Spirit has worked in individual lives and in the church as a whole in the past.

Naturally *the* model life for the church is that of her Lord Jesus Christ. There have been, however, those throughout history in whom the Spirit has worked in such a way that their imitation of Christ had a powerful effect both on their contemporaries and on the church that came after them. These "saints" as the Catholics call them or "spiritual giants" as the Protestants refer to them may have a continuing ministry in the church today. We need to remember their courage in the faith and devotion to our Lord as an ever-present encouragement in our midst. The reading of Athanasius' *On The Incarnation*, Augustine's *Confessions*, Bernard of Clairvaux's *The Steps of Humility*, Thomas à Kempis' *The*

---

[4]For development of this notion, see Lawrence O. Richards, *A Theology of Christian Education* (Grand Rapids: Zondervan, 1975).

Imitation of Christ, or John Bunyan's *Pilgrim's Progress* certainly continue to speak today, and reading and studying them cannot but help communicate growth in Christ.

Second, *nurture is modeled in the social context of the church.* Because the church is a visible and tangible community within society, each local congregation provides a social context in which the believer is nurtured. Communication of the life of Christ occurs as the local body seeks to incarnate the life of Christ in her midst. The relationships within this community ought to reflect the triune relationships as the body is drawn into union with God. Consequently there are two considerations that must be kept in mind:

(1) The impersonal church denies the presence of the triune God in her midst. Where God is, there one will find warm and caring personal relationships.

(2) Not everyone in a local body will be on the same growth level. A healthy congregation consists of those who have matured in Christ, those who are new in Christ, and those who are in the process of turning from habits of sin toward a more complete imitation of Christ. For this reason a Christian community must learn to accept people where they are and nurture them along toward growth in Christ within the community.

The church is the household of God; and when it is seen as that, it has that sense of family in which the process of growth is both tolerated and encouraged.

Third, *nurture is modeled in the church's vision of the future.* The vision always held before the church is that of the kingdom. Even as Israel looked for the fulfillment of the promise and lived in expectation, so the church lives in the anticipation of the consummation and the realization of the new heavens and the new earth. The Holy Spirit is at work now in the church, shaping the church for its ultimate union with God. This hope is the hope of the church, which is her goal as well. It must be kept alive in the life of the church now as a means of nurturing her growth into Christ.

For example, a troubled friend wrote to me saying that it was painful for her to take the Lord's Supper because of her broken marriage. Should she celebrate the sign of our reconciliation with

God and our fellowman when she herself was not reconciled to her husband? Was she making a sham of the Eucharist?

I wrote to her and explained how the Lord's Supper expresses both the *fact* of our reconciliation (accomplished by Christ) and the *goal* of our behavior. The point is that reconciliation is not yet a fully realized experience. It is a fact that we have been reconciled before God, but that reconciliation is in the process of being worked out in our earthly pilgrimage. It is a *goal*. We are moving toward the total reconciliation of all things, and the Eucharist is a sign of our goal and a means of nurturing us in the attainment of it.

We conclude, then, that the Holy Spirit acts as an Agent in the church, using the gifts of ministry and fruits of the Spirit within the historical, social, and eschatalogical aspects of the church as a means by which believers are nurtured in their growth in Christ.

COMMUNICATING GROWTH WITHIN THE CHURCH

I have argued that growth in Christ occurs within the church as the nurturing community. Because growth takes place in the context of community rather than in isolation, the communal nature of Christian learning needs to be recognized. We will look then at the *process of learning*, which takes place in the Christian community as the church communicates the *meaning* of the Christian faith and the *experience* of the Christian faith.

Communicating the Meaning of the Christian Faith

An interesting question is raised in Deuteronomy 6. It appears that God Himself is raising the question in Moses' mind. The situation is this: God foresees the descendents of the Israelites raising doubts about the meaning and significance of the religious character of the nation. So He says,

> "When your son asks you in time to come saying, 'What do the testimonies and the statutes and the judgments mean which the Lord commanded you?' then you shall say to your son, 'We were slaves to Pharaoh in Egypt; and the Lord brought us from Egypt with a mighty hand. Moreover the Lord showed great and

distressing signs and wonders before our eyes against Egypt, Pharaoh and all his household; and He brought us out from there in order to bring us in, to give us the land which He had sworn to our fathers.' "So the LORD commanded us to observe all these statutes, to fear the LORD our God for our good always and for our survival, as it is today. And it will be righteousness for us if we are careful to observe all this commandment before the LORD our God, just as He commanded us" (Deut. 6:20–25).

The answer God gave the Israelite fathers was one of recounting Israel's pilgrimage from Egypt through the wilderness and into the promised land. Because God is a God who works in history and within a social context, He reveals Himself through the events of life, particularly those that belong to the people of God. God communicates in the context of the life of the community. If we would communicate the meaning of the Christian faith, we would do well to follow the pattern that God has established.

The meaning of the Christian faith is never fully understood apart from an understanding of the life of God's people in the world.

If we would communicate the Christian faith we must recover an ability to recite what God has done in history. This includes not only the exodus event and the life of Israel, the incarnation event and the life of the early church, but an understanding of the people of God in her two-thousand-year pilgrimage.

It is important to know something about God's ways with His church. There is a need to recover Christian roots, to stand in the stream of the church throughout history.

The Holy Spirit may communicate to us through the Bible alone and sometimes does. Nevertheless the Holy Spirit is in inseparable union with the church and speaks through her to us. We need to know what the Holy Spirit has been saying to the church throughout her history! In this way the church *hands down* the meaning of the Christian faith.

Communicating the Experience of the Christian Faith

If it is the meaning of the Christian faith and not just knowledge about the faith that we wish to communicate, then we must ask how that meaning is conveyed. An interesting hint is given to us in Deuteronomy 6 in the instruction God gave to Moses.

> "These words, which I command you this day, shall be on your heart; and you shall teach them diligently to your sons and shall talk of them when you sit in your house and when you walk by the way and when you lie down and when you rise up. And you shall bind them as a sign on your hand and they shall be as frontals on your forehead. And you shall write them on the doorposts of your house and on your gates" (Deut. 6:6–9).

It is clear from an examination of the words that the emphasis falls on *experiencing truth in the context of life*. That truth, which is in the heart, must be there when you *sit, walk, lie down, and rise*. Truth is to be everywhere in the context of living—on your hand, frontals on your forehead, on the doorposts of your house and on the gates. The point is that the meaning of truth is realized through the experience of truth. Truth is confirmed by the doing of truth.

If the church is, as we have argued, the new humanity and therefore the context in which growth is to occur, it is the responsibility of the church to provide an atmosphere in which the Christian faith is made real through experience.[5] The question then with which we have to deal is this: What spiritual means does the church have at her disposal for communicating the experience of faith and thereby fostering growth in her members?

The answer to this question lies in the direction of recognizing the church as a community that reenacts the events from which it derives its meaning.[6] Those historical events that give meaning to the church are repeated over and over again; and through them, by the power of the Holy Spirit, the experience of the Christian faith is handed down.

[5]See Lawrence O. Richards, "Church Teaching: Content Without Context," *Christianity Today* (April 15, 1977).
[6]See John Navone, S.J., "The Gospel Truth as Re-enactment," *Scottish Journal of Theology*, vol. 29, pp. 311–33.

From a theological standpoint it looks like this: God sent His eternal Son, the Word that became flesh in the Person of Jesus Christ. Jesus communicated the Father by His physical presence, His speaking, and His life, death, and resurrection. Christ in turn instructed His church to communicate Himself by *her* life—by the word she speaks, the life she lives, the hope she bears. This is the job for which He sent the Holy Spirit to empower us to do. Therefore, as the church reenacts the life of Christ in her, she *communicates* Christ. For Christ is not absent from the church, but is present in the church. In this sense the church hands down Jesus Christ. The church is the context in which Jesus Christ is continually communicated in the believer, and even to the world.

Growth in Christ is especially enhanced by specific ministries within the church. *In and through the God-ordained activities of the church, communication occurs; growth results when the believer participates in these activities by faith.* Several examples follow.

Worship. Worship is one way through which a significant transfer of events from one generation to the next takes place. Worship transfers events through *recitation* and *rehearsal*.

The service of the Word, which consists of reading Scripture and preaching, is an oral recitation of those past events that continue to give meaning to our lives today. A good communicator in reading and preaching is one who can make the events of the past come alive. Preaching re-creates the event and brings it to us by the power of speech. The Holy Spirit works through that proclamation in such a way that the hearer experiences the original event and therefore reacts to it in a way similar to those who were actual witnesses.

In the same way the service of the Lord's Supper *rehearses* the main event of the Christian faith. The elements of bread and wine, the table of the Lord, the words of institution, the blessing, the breaking, the giving, and the receiving are all part of the enactment through which a real and substantial communication occurs.

Participation in worship is not meant to be rote or casual. It requires an active I'm-really-there-with-Christ approach. It is something the church *does*, not something the church observes. In this sense, doing the Eucharist *is* a ritual.[7] In the Eucharist one goes through certain motions, observable movements that are determined by the meaning of what is happening.

The meaning of what is happening is, of course, rooted in the actual historical event. But the experience of that meaningful event is now being re-created in the worship of the church. By going through the ritual *in faith*, the believer is using his mind, body, emotions, and senses to ascribe worth to God and to thank Him for redemption. At the same time his senses are opened to God's grace. A two-way communication occurs between man and God.

Baptism (or Dedication). The occasion when a child or an adult is brought into the Christian community creates an opportunity for the whole congregation to renew their initial commitment to Christ.

Entrance into the church is replete with Christian symbolism (as seen in the previous chapter). These gestures and actions are all means through which communication may occur, particularly if the congregation is aware of their meanings.

Because baptism is the passage way into the church, every baptism is a reminder of each believer's own baptism. In the ancient church it became customary for the whole body to prepare for baptism with the initiates. The baptized believer did not go through the entire preparation but participated in some of the final preparations, particularly the final fastings and the all-night vigil (in the case of Easter baptisms). The vigil consisted of a series of Scripture readings that recount the creation and re-creation of the world and the salvation of man through Christ. Then, when the convert was baptized into Christ and the church, the whole Christian community repeated their baptismal vows to signify their own recommitment to Christ and His church.

In today's church, baptism is too often something we watch. There is a great need to return to baptism as a means not only of bringing new people into the church but of restoring our relation-

---

[7]See Edward A. Fischer, "Ritual as Communication," *Worship*, vol. 45, no. 2, pp. 73–91.

ship to God through the communication of the meaning of baptism for everyone in the community.

Confirmation (or Rededication). In the ancient church, confirmation, or Chrism (from the Greek *charis,* meaning "gift" or "grace") was the rite of receiving the Holy Spirit.

Originally the rite was performed immediately after baptism. In the course of time, however, due partially to the practice of infant baptism, confirmation was separated from baptism and became a rite administered in early adulthood.

In Protestant churches today we observe a similar practice. The Baptists dedicate their children and later put them through a period of instruction followed by baptism. The Presbyterians baptize their children and later teach them the catechism, which is then followed by full membership in the church. Even the Wesleyan and Pentecostal belief in a second blessing reminds one of the ancient church practice. Of course, the call to rededication within the fundamentalist and evangelical groups draws on the same tradition.

The point is that maturation in Christ is not only a matter of steady growth but also one of dramatic turning points. There are times when we encounter God in unusual ways. These times ought not to be isolated from the church but be a very part of the church so that our growth occurs in the context of the living community of believers.[8]

Traditionally, confirmation (or the reception of the Holy Spirit) was attended by three signs: the laying on of hands, an anointing of oil, and a signing on the forehead with the sign of the cross.

The laying on of hands is an ancient symbol which originated in the Old Testament, was used by Jesus, and was employed by the apostles to signify the conferral of a blessing.

The anointing with oil signified the giving of the Spirit. The external sign points to the inner anointing of the Spirit. (This is sometimes put so strongly that the Spirit Himself is described as

[8]See Bernard J. Cooke, S.J., *Christian Sacraments and Christian Personality* (New York: Doubleday, 1965).

the anointing.) The anointing with oil specifically emphasized the bestowal of the gift of the Spirit.

The signing of the cross on the forehead symbolized dedication to Christ. It pointed to man's identity with Christ as a soldier who is branded for duty. It was similar to the formalizing of a contract.

If the church today desires to grow in Christ, more consideration should be given to dramatic turning points in the Christian life. This may be accomplished both by placing an emphasis on these significant events and by the restored use of symbolism as a nonverbal form of communication.

Confession. If faith, as we have defined it in Chapter 3, is a matter of hearing the Word of God in such a way that it produces awareness of God (and His claim on our life and the life of the world) and obedience to what we have heard, then there must be an opportunity in the Christian life for the ongoing application of the Word to one's life. It is in the practice of confession where spiritual scrutiny (attended by a turning away from sin and turning toward God) fosters growth in Christ.[9]

Christian psychology recognizes the need for confession in personal growth. Confession is part of the process of redemption, a response-forming process that helps a person *act* out the goal of a Christian lifestyle. For this reason confession ought to be accompanied by an expiation that allows the believer not only to turn away from his sin but also to turn toward his new life in Christ.

Professor Hobart Mowrer explains the significance of expiation this way:

> People do not merely talk themselves into sin; they *act*. And by the same token, I do not believe anyone ever talks himself *out* of sin. Again there must be action, and this action must involve not only confession, of an ultimately open type, but also atonement. Confession without a sober program of expiation can be dangerous, in the sense of causing the individual to be overwhelmed with guilt and self-hatred.[10]

[9]See John R.W. Stott, *Confess Your Sins: The Way of Reconciliation* (Philadelphia: Westminster Press, 1965).
[10]Hobart Mowrer, *Learning Theory and Personality Dynamics* (New York: Ronald Press Co., 1950), p. 601.

In the history of the Christian church there are two kinds of confession: public and private. The Reformation churches have incorporated into their worship a form of public confession. It is usually a brief statement, recognizing sin and confessing it to the Lord followed by a statement recognizing the forgiveness of sin provided by God through Jesus Christ. However, public confession is general and does not offer an opportunity to reflect on actual personal sins. In other words there is not a real *grappling* with sin in one's own life in public confession. Therefore, perhaps we need to reinstate some form of private confession.

I believe there is a crying need to restore a pastoral concern for the "cure of souls." Pastoral care is not the exclusive responsibility of the minister. The renewal movements in our day, particularly the charismatic renewal, have given the gift of "hearing a confession" back to the congregation. The gift of prescribing a course of action to help a person actualize the life of Christ belongs to the whole church.

If we are concerned to communicate growth in Christ, then we ought to consider a return to private confession as a way of dealing with guilt and releasing persons to continued growth in Christian character.

Professor Emeritus of pastoral ministries at Asbury Seminary, Curry Mavis, says:

> Guilt feelings are debilitating because they cause one to look backward instead of forward. In doing this they obscure objectives with a loss of motivation. . . . Furthermore, guilt feelings are spiritually disabling because they produce anxiety. Anxiety is a psychic and spiritual crippler, as paralysis is to the body. It destroys initiative through a morbid fear of failure.[11]

Because guilt holds a person back from growth, there is a need for forgiveness. In forgiveness God redirects our energies and turns a self-destructive guilt-ridden person into a constructive person whose energies may now be channeled toward becoming a new person in Christ.

I have not attempted to provide an exhaustive list of those

[11]Curry W. Mavis, *The Psychology of Christian Experience* (Grand Rapids: Zondervan, 1963), p. 27.

activities within the Christian community that stimulate growth. Much needs to be said about the ministries God gives to each of us in the body. We are all called to be ministers to each other, to employ our gifts within the body for the building up of each other. It should be the concern of each Christian community to provide a free atmosphere in which persons are able to both offer their gifts and receive the gifts of others. When a Christian community expects the minister to be the only minister, it is doomed to fail. Growth occurs through *doing*; and when those who can minister in the body are ministering, the transformation of life in the context of the body is maximized.

CONCLUSION

My concern in this chapter has been to discuss growth in Christ in the church. Let me recapitulate.

In the first place, I argued for growth in four areas:

- The goal of the church should be knowledge, which leads to understanding and wisdom.
- The goal of the church should be to develop attitudes that are Christian and universal, not subcultural and parochial.
- The goal of the church should be to communicate patterns of behavior that model biblical values.
- The goal of the church is to provide an atmosphere in which the gifts of Christian ministry given to all the members may flourish.

In the second place, I argued that growth in the Christian life occurs best in the context of the church as a community:

- The church is in inseparable union with the Holy Spirit. The task of the Holy Spirit is to communicate the life of Christ in His body.
- The church is best perceived as a nurturing community. Each local community may draw from the history of the church, the present social context of the living community, and the vision of the future.

In the third place, I discussed *how* growth may occur within the church:

- To begin, we must concern ourselves to communicate the meaning of the Christian faith, not merely facts about the faith.

- The meaning of the faith is best communicated through the experience of the faith. This communication occurs within the life of the church, especially in worship, baptism (or dedication), confirmation (or re-dedication), confession, and the ministries of the body.

The point we must keep in mind is that God speaks through the church. The church, His body, is inseparably linked with Christ through the Holy Spirit. For this reason a vertical and horizontal communication between God and His church and among the people within the church is continuous. We need to recover both the sense of this action and the experience of it in our midst.

11
RECOVERING MISSION

In the last two chapters we examined ways to communicate *within* the church. Now let's turn our attention to communication by the church to the world.

These are the questions we need to ask: What is the relationship of the church to the world? How can the church actually communicate to the world? The emphasis, therefore, is not on how *I* can communicate to the world, but on how *the church as a corporate organism, a society of believers, can communicate to the world through her very presence in the world.*

We have already defined what is meant by the church. The church is the people of God who constitute the new creation. She is characterized as a fellowship of faith, the body of Christ. As such, she is an instrument of the kingdom of God and a witness to it. In short she is the presence of the future in the world, here and now.

Before we can discuss the relationship of the church to the world, however, we must define the word *world.* Because there are a number of different usages of the word *world* in the Scriptures, we must be careful to state precisely what we mean by the word.

THE MEANINGS OF *WORLD*

It must be recognized that the word *world*, which comes from the Greek word *kosmos*, is used in a *number of different ways.*[1]

---

[1]For a detailed examination of *kosmos* see Gerhard Kittel, ed., *Theological Dictionary of the New Testament*, vol. 3 (Grand Rapids: Eerdmans, 1965).

Sometimes it is used as a synonym for the Old Testament phrase "heaven and earth." This is a broad usage, a spatial sense in which everything that is, is included. A more narrow use of *kosmos* designates the physical world, the earth. This usage may refer to material possession of the things of the earth, as in Jesus' statement: "For what will it profit a man if he gains the whole world, and loses his own soul?" (Mark 8:36).

A further narrowing of the word brings it down to *humanity*. For example, Jesus used the word in this manner several times. He told His disciples "You are the light of the world" (Matt. 5:14). Later, He cautioned them "woe to the world for offenses [temptations to sin]!" (Matt. 18:7). These statements are obviously not directed toward the universe, nor toward the physical world, but toward humanity. Jesus could have said, "You are the light of humanity."

World is sometimes used to refer to the *place where salvation occurs*. Both the apostles Paul and John understood the word this way. John wrote, "We have seen and testify that the Father has sent the Son as Savior of the world" (1 John 4:14). This usage of *world* comes into clearer focus through Paul's comparison of the spirit of the world with the Spirit of God. "Now we have received, not the spirit of the world, but the Spirit who is from God . . ." (1 Cor. 2:12; see also 1 Cor. 1:20,21).

In this way the New Testament writers created the connotation that *the world stands in antithesis to God*. This does not refer to the material or physical world but to the spirit of the world. The origin of the spirit of the world is traced back to sin: "Therefore as by one man sin entered into the world, and death by sin, and thus death spread to all men, because all sinned" (Rom. 5:12). The consequence of sin is that the world stands under judgment (see Rom. 3:6,19).

An important consideration, however, is that *God is victorious over the world*. ". . . God was in Christ reconciling the world to Himself, not imputing their trespasses to them" (2 Cor. 5:19). This means the spirit of the world and its effect on humanity and on the creation will be destroyed at the consummation.

However, we need not wait until the consummation to enter into God's victory. The Christian is released from the power of the world *now*. Because Christ has overcome the world in His death and resurrection, *the Christian has the power to exercise the victory of Christ over evil in the world.*

Paul set forth this motif in Colossians 1:13: "He has delivered us from the power of darkness and translated us into the kingdom of the Son of His love." Paul was more precise in Galatians 1:3,4: ". . . our Lord Jesus Christ, who gave Himself for our sins, that He might deliver us from this present evil age," and in Ephesians 2:1,2: "And you He has made alive, who were dead in trespasses and sins, in which you once walked according to the course of this world, according to the prince of the power of the air, the spirit who now works in the sons of disobedience."

What Paul was describing is the church. The church is not to be of the spirit of the world because the church is of Christ and Christ has overcome the spirit of the world.

In our consideration, then, of how the church communicates to the world, we can see that there are at least three levels to which this question must be addressed. First, we must consider how the church is part of the world (i.e., the created order). Second, we must probe the stance of the church toward the world (i.e., the spirit of the world). Third, we need to define the role of the church in her victory over the world (i.e., the world reconciled).[2]

THE CHURCH IN THE WORLD

There are two ways the church belongs to, or relates to, the world.

In the first place, the world is *the sphere of the church's operation.* It is in time, space, and history that her life is lived. John described this level when he wrote, ". . . as He is, so are we in this world" (1 John 4:17). Jesus also recognized the continuance of the church in the world in His prayer at Gethsemane. He prayed, "And now I am no longer in the world, but these are in the world, and I come to You" (John 17:11). In the same prayer He said, "I do

[2]See a similar approach in Hendrik Kraemer, *The Communication of the Christian Faith* (Philadelphia: Westminster Press, 1956), ch. 2 ("Communication in the History of the Church").

not pray that You take them out of the world, but that You keep them from the evil one" (John 17:15).

In these statements Jesus acknowledged the existence of the church in the world where the powers of evil still rage and carry out their destructive purposes. The church cannot help but rub up against, relate to, and be affected by the continual presence of the enemy. We know from the history of the church that when the church has not adequately stood against evil powers, they have made their way into the church and weakened her witness to the world. The church must, therefore, always be on guard against a toleration of evil or a mere co-habitation with the powers. The church cannot afford to be neutral.

The second way the church is related to the world is significantly different from the way we've just discussed. *The church sustains a redemptive relationship with the world (the created order)*. This idea emphasizes the biblical notion that both the church and the creation have been redeemed. The relationship of the church to the world in this case is contained in the concept of a cosmic redemption.

Paul spoke to this issue in his letter to the Colossian Christians. He connected creation and redemption, telling them that Christ is Creator of all things "in heaven and . . . on earth, visible and invisible, whether thrones or dominions or principalities or powers" (Col. 1:16). In the same section he told them that "it pleased the Father that in Him [Christ] all fullness should dwell, and by Him to reconcile all things to Himself, by Him, whether things on earth or things in heaven, having made peace through the blood of His cross" (Col. 1:19,20).

What Paul was emphasizing here was the redemption of the created order as well as the redemption of humanity through the work of Jesus Christ. He described this more fully to the Roman Christians: "the creation itself . . . will be delivered from the bondage of corruption into the glorious liberty of the children of God" (Rom. 8:21). He went on to say that "the whole creation groans and labors with birth pangs together until now; and not only they, but ourselves also who have the firstfruits of the Spirit, even we ourselves groan within ourselves, eagerly waiting for the adoption, the redemption of our body" (Rom. 8:21–23).

It is clear from these passages that both the church and the created order have been redeemed by the work of Christ on the cross. This redemption, however, will not be completed until the consummation. In the meantime both the church and the creation "wait for it with perseverance" (Rom. 8:25). Clearly, then, there is a relationship here between the church and the world that needs to be more fully probed. How does the church, we may ask, communicate her redemption and the redemption of the created order to the world of humanity?

The answer to this question does not lie in oral communication but in communication through action. Because the church is a *visible* part of the world, and therefore inextricably interwoven not only with the physical and social environment but also, and more significantly, with the *structure of meaning*, the action of the church as a means of communicating the gospel is of great significance.[3] What the church does and how she acts and behaves in society communicates what she is in her internal essence. When the church fights and divides, she communicates one thing; when she displays love and unity and reaches out around her to bring healing into the structures of society and to provide direction and hope for a confused world, she communicates another thing.

Because the church is the redeemed community, her task and function in the world is to communicate the meaning of redemption as it relates to every area of life. In this respect there are two considerations to keep in mind.

Reciprocal Relationship

Because the church is in the world (i.e. in the created order) she is *intimately bound to the world in a reciprocal type of relationship*. For this reason the church, both the world-wide church and the local church, sustains an undeniable relationship to the natural creation and society at large. Whether the church is indifferent, negative, or positive toward a particular issue is a matter of communication. In Nazi Germany, for example, the established

---

[3]See Philip Hefner, "Ecological Perspectives on Communicating the Gospel," *Lutheran World*, vol. 16, no. 4 (1969), pp. 322–38.

church communicated one thing by its support of the Third Reich. The confessing church, on the other hand, communicated another message by its opposition.

Today our world is confronted by staggering problems: the problem of hunger in two thirds of the world and overabundance in the other one third; the loss of meaning through technology; the rise of crime; the energy crisis; corruption in politics; the breakdown of morality; the rapid rise of divorce and the attending problem of broken homes and dislocated people; the problems of abortion, homosexuality, euthanasia; and a host of other matters that confront us daily in the newspaper and on television.

What the church universal and local does about these problems communicates significantly to the world. We must avoid the extremes: On the one hand, the church sometimes falls into the trap of acting like a mere social institution; on the other hand, the church sometimes retreats altogether from the issues at hand and ignores them, concentrating on the personal purity and morality of its members.

The church is called neither to secularized social actions nor to indifference. Her message is one of a new creation: A new beginning has occurred in Jesus Christ, the Cosmic Redeemer. This new beginning is both for man and for the created order. When the church acts redemptively within the structures of creation and society, she cannot help but speak and act in such a way that she points to the redemption of all things in Christ. That is, she can lead the way toward the future because she alone has the vision of the future.

This kind of collective communication is a powerful witness in the world. The church is beginning to awaken to this task, but still has a long way to go toward reaching the goal of effective communication.

Unconscious Communication

Second, *the presence of the church in the world establishes an unconscious communication.* This aspect of communication is more difficult to determine than the more obvious expression of the church detailed above.

I remember, for example, the impression the church in Russia made on me in a recent visit to that country. In Moscow, as well as in other cities of Russia and in the countryside, the golden domes of the Byzantine churches can be seen. I climbed the steeple of one of the main churches in Moscow and looked out over the skyline, ablaze with the golden domes of hundreds of churches. Although many of those churches were closed, the very existence of the buildings and the special use of space made by them spoke to me of the way in which the Christian message had permeated (and was still present) in the very layout of this large Russian city.

No one can walk through a Russian city, read Russian literature, listen to Russian music, or look at Russian art without being confronted by a sense of the holy. While this is particularly and obviously true in Russia, it is also true of medieval Europe and its inseparable Christian character, the remnants of which can still be seen in Western culture.

Recently, in the United States, and generally in the West, the secularization of society has made a more significant unconscious impact than has the church. The church has to a certain extent retreated from art, literature, music, and architecture. The retreat of the church from the world has signaled an unconscious rejection of cosmic redemption, and in its place an individualistic, privatistic Christianity has emerged. The secular society, not the church and her cosmic vision, appears to be the most formative unconscious communicator of our time in the West, and perhaps around the world.

I am advocating that the church communicate to the world through her very *presence* in the world. If this concept were taken more seriously, we would see a much deeper concern on the part of Christians to make a cultural impact. We would begin to think more deeply about the redemptive impact of church architecture, Christian art, Christian music, and Christian literature.

When the church is alive and doing well, in the sense of fulfilling her vocation as a redemptive presence, the influence of the church in the world is inescapable. It is impossible to calculate the exact impact the church makes in the world through her presence. Often without conscious effort the church helps shape the values of society and makes a socioeconomic impact. When she accepts her mission to the world and *actively* engages in making her presence known, the positive impact on the structures of society is proportionately increased.

We turn now to examine the more conscious effort the church makes against evil.

THE CHURCH IS NOT OF
THE SPIRIT OF THE WORLD

Both Paul and John speak of *kosmos* in a personified way. The world is the great enemy of Christ. It is the world that "did not know Him" (John 1:10), the world Paul described as "principalities," "powers," "the rulers of the darkness of this age," "spiritual wickedness in the heavenly places" (Eph. 6:12). This is the world that hates Christ as He Himself said: ". . . it hates Me because I testify of it that its works are evil" (John 7:7). The world also hates the church because, as Jesus said, ". . . I have chosen you out of the world, therefore the world hates you" (John 15:19).

This world, the world of evil powers, greed, hate, violence, lust, immorality, murder is the world Christ has judged. To the crowd that came to hear Him after they had heard of His raising Lazarus from the dead, Jesus said, "Now is the judgment of this world; now the ruler of this world will be cast out" (John 12:31, cf. John 16:11, 14:30). Paul, interpreting Christ's death, wrote, "Having disarmed principalities and powers, He made a public spectacle of them, triumphing over them in it" (Col. 2:15).

Therefore, even though "the whole world lies in the power of the wicked one" (1 John 5:19), Jesus, because of His death and resurrection, was able to say, ". . . be of good cheer, I have overcome the world" (John 16:33). In the same way John encouraged the church in her struggle against evil, recognizing that "He who is in you is greater than he who is in the world" (1 John 4:4).

For this reason the church is not of the world. Jesus said, "I have chosen you out of the world . . ." (John 15:19) and then compared the relationship of the church toward the world with His own relationship to the world. He said, ". . . the world has hated them because they are not of the world, even as I am not of the world" (John 17:14).

The stance of the church toward the world is therefore quite clear. Paul wrote, "Do not be conformed to this world . . ." (Rom. 12:2). He urged the church to "use this world as not abusing it" (1 Cor. 7:31). James also reminded the Christians "that friendship with the world is enmity with God . . . Whoever therefore wants to be a friend of the world makes himself an enemy of God" (James 4:4). John is no less clear, cautioning the church to "not love the world or the things in the world. If any one loves the world, the love of the Father is not in him. For all that is in the world—the lust of the flesh, the lust of the eyes, and the pride of life—is not of the Father but is of the world" (1 John 2:15,16).

It is clear from the teaching of the New Testament that *the church is called to take an active stance against the world, against the powers of evil.* The question is: How does the church communicate her stance against the powers?[4]

Evangelism

In the first place the church is called to fulfill the great commission. Jesus said, "You will receive power when the Holy Spirit has come upon you; and you will be witnesses to Me . . ." (Acts 1:8). The church is commissioned to "make disciples of all the nations" (Matt. 28:19). It is her responsibility to preach the word of reconciliation, to declare Christ's victory over evil, and to invite people to renounce their allegiance to sin and to follow Jesus in His church.

This commission cannot be replaced or fall into disuse. It is still the *primary* means of spreading the gospel. Our concern for Christian architecture, music, art, and literature dare not replace the significance of *personal* witness to the power of Christ.

It is, of course, not a matter of either/or but of both/and. It does seem to be difficult to maintain the balance. Some shy away from personal evangelism but throw themselves into a less direct form

---

[4]For a treatment of the special role of the church in America, see William Stringfellow, *An Ethic for Christians and Other Aliens in a Strange Land* (Waco, Tex.: Word Books, 1973).

of communicating the gospel. Others, who put all their efforts into personal evangelism frequently disdain the less direct attempts to speak to the world.

It would be well to remember that both are needed and that both are expressed in the church when the church is seen as a whole. One part of the church may be exercising the gift of evangelism more than another. Nevertheless the whole church is acting through that group. The gift, therefore, belongs to the whole body and not to a part. For this reason we must seek to become more mutually supportive of those whose gifts complement ours.

The Prophetic Stance

If the church is going to communicate to the world that she is indeed against the powers, the voice of one or two will seldom be heard. On the other hand, denominational or local church pronouncements are equally inadequate.

What is needed is a better approach: *the prophetic stance*. The prophet calls for an application of the Word of God to the very life-structure of society. The prophetic voice challenges the permeation of evil in society and its expression within the institutions of man. Like Amos, the prophetic voice calls: "But let justice roll down like waters/And righteousness like an ever-flowing stream" (Amos 5:24).

The prophetic stance is not only a voice but also an alternative lifestyle. The church is called to live in such a way that she expresses her freedom from worldly domination and bondage. She is an organism of people expressing a new fabric of human relationships, modeled on a commitment to a lifestyle that sharply contrasts with the world's. Her power is the power of service, not of domination.[5]

Although the whole church is called to live this way, often the church as an institution allows herself to be controlled by the

---

[5]For an example of a local church that has attempted to make these principles concrete, see the study of Church of the Redeemer in Houston, Texas, as detailed by W. Graham Pulkingham, *They Left Their Nets* (New York: Morehouse-Barlow, 1973), and *Gathered for Power* (New York: Morehouse-Barlow, 1972).

powers she is called to be against. This often calls forth a strong counter-movement, which provides a stark, and sometimes excessive, contrast to the established church and to the society at large. The monastic movement functions in this way, and so do the new communities emerging here and there as visible witnesses to the other-worldly character of the church.

It is important for the people of God not to invalidate these witnesses, for they provide by their very existence a communication of the church's stance against the powers. Their existence in the world speaks loudly to the world and to the powers that control the world. God speaks through the church as she stands against the world. We cannot and must not fail to communicate this word of witness.

The Catachetical Method

A third way the church speaks against the world is in the use of *the catachetical method.* In this approach, the church inculcates morality by teaching. This is a method that takes place within the church but finds expression in the action of the church in the world.

Philip Carrington, in his work *The Primitive Christian Catechism,* has effectively although not conclusively, shown that much of the New Testament material is set forth according to an ancient catachetical model.[6]

The approach sets forth two ways: The *way of life* and the *way of death.* The choice between alternatives is made clear and each person may choose one or the other. The contrast sets them in bold relief so that the antithesis is clear. There is no in-between gray area.

For example, in Romans 6 Paul wrote, ". . . you are that one's servants whom you obey, whether of sin to death, or of obedience to righteousness . . ." (Rom. 6:16). He spelled this out more clearly in a catalogue of sins in Galatians and Colossians. He called these the "works of the flesh" and listed "adultery, fornication, uncleanness, licentiousness, idolatry, sorcery, hatred, con-

---

[6]Philip Carrington, *The Primitive Christian Catechism* (Cambridge: University Press, 1940).

tention, jealousy, outbursts of wrath, selfish ambition, dissensions, heresies, envy, murders, drunkenness, revelry, and the like . . ." (Gal. 5:19–21). To the Colossians he cited similar evils and then called on these Christians to put away "anger, wrath, malice, blasphemy, filthy language out of your mouth" (Col. 3:8). These are examples of what the church is against.

THE CHURCH IN CHRIST IS VICTORIOUS OVER THE WORLD

The third relationship the church sustains with the world is rooted in the victory over sin and death accomplished by Christ in His death and resurrection and coming consummation.

This relationship is presented in a number of somewhat complex levels in the New Testament. In the first place, *it is clear through the preaching and teaching of Jesus that He has overcome evil powers*. He said to His disciples, "In the world you will have tribulation; but be of good cheer, I have overcome the world" (John 16:33). Paul interpreted Christ's death as a victory over the powers of evil. "Having disarmed principalities and powers," Paul wrote, "He made a public spectacle of them, triumphing over them in it" (Col. 2:15).

It is equally clear that *the effect of sin in nature and the power of sin over man has been defeated*. Death, that power of disintegration over man and the created order, has been destroyed by the power of Christ's death and resurrection. As Paul stated, "When this corruptible has put on incorruption, and this mortal has put on immortality, then shall be brought to pass the saying that is written: "Death is swallowed up in victory./O death, where is your sting?/O Hades, where is your victory?" (1 Cor. 15:54,55).

The death of Christ releases from death not only man but also the entire creation. "The creation itself also will be delivered from the bondage of corruption . . ." (Rom. 8:21). Both man and the created order, therefore, no longer need follow "the course of this world," but are now "alive together with Christ" (see Eph. 2:2–10). Thus, together with the creation we are "eagerly waiting for the adoption, the redemption of our body" (Rom. 8:23). This anticipation by the redeemed (both humanity and creation), points to the consummation where the final accomplishment of redemption will occur.

Another aspect of Christ's victory over the world as seen in the church has to do with the presence of the church in history. She lives, as noted earlier, between the resurrection and the consummation, in the time between Pentecost and the second coming. In this context she is to express her mission, which is to carry on the work of Christ, thus overcoming the world. Jesus indicated this relationship in His prayer: "As You have sent Me into the world, I also have sent them into the world" (John 17:18).

The apostle John commented on this motif when he wrote, "For whatever is born of God overcomes the world. And this is the victory that has overcome the world—our faith" (1 John 5:4,5). Paul emphasized this aspect of the church's mission in his letter to the Corinthians: ". . . God was in Christ reconciling the world to Himself . . . and has committed to us the word of reconciliation. Therefore we are ambassadors for Christ, as though God were pleading by us . . ." (2 Cor. 5:19,20).

All these considerations point to a relationship between the church and the world in which *the church applies the redemption of Christ to the world*. Because Christ is victorious over the world, the church, which is the body of Christ, is called to exercise Christ's victory over the world *now*.

This calling of the church in the world is not only affirmed by the teachings of Christ and Paul as noted above, but also by the whole structure of biblical revelation. The doctrine of creation affirms the basic goodness of the world. It teaches that there is order, purpose, and meaning in the world and that the world belongs to God, even though it is the realm of Satan's activity due to the fall. The incarnation affirms the goodness of creation again since God in Christ became like His creatures.

By taking on a created human body and spirit, Jesus Christ took upon Himself the same death and disintegration that affects the entire created order. In His death and resurrection He redeemed the created order from the effects of sin. He reversed the order of sin and death and re-created His own creation. Now Christ continues His presence in the world through the church by the power of the Holy Spirit. The church, which stands by the power of the resurrection, anticipates the consummation when the work of Christ will be completed and all things will be made whole.

The victory of Christ over the world and His victorious presence in the church raises this question: How is the church to communicate Christ's victory over the world?

Preaching

The first and most obvious means of communicating the victory of Christ is through preaching. Paul stressed the importance of preaching in his letter to the Romans. "How then shall they call Him in whom they have not believed? And how shall they believe in Him of whom they have not heard? And how shall they hear without a preacher?" (Rom. 10:14).

The word *preach*, as explained in Chapter 3, does not mean to explain or moralize but *to announce and proclaim*. The church has a joyful announcement to make to the world—man and the created order have been released from the power of sin and set free. Paul wrote, "knowing this, that our old man was crucified with Him, that the body of sin might be done away with, that we should no longer serve sin" (Rom. 6:6). For this reason he could go on to write the bold and glorious words; "For he who has died has been freed from sin" (Rom. 6:8).

A major problem with preachers and with preaching today is a lack of understanding, a failure to see the message as a message of *victory* and the method of proclaiming it as an *announcement*. We can scarcely communicate that which we don't understand. As troublesome as that is, it becomes even more difficult when we garble the message into a mere belief system or a calling to moral awareness. The message we communicate has to do with both belief and morals, but they arise out of the announcement of Christ's victory over evil, which can be experienced in and through the life of the church.

Power of the Holy Spirit

A second way to communicate Christ's victory over evil is to experience the power of Christ over evil through the ministry of the Holy Spirit.

In the ancient church Christ's victory over sin was proclaimed in the Eucharist and experienced in eating the bread and drinking the wine. Ignatius (A.D. 110) wrote to the Ephesians, commending them to "break one loaf, which is the medicine of immortality, and the antidote which wards off death but yields continuous life in union with Jesus Christ."[7]

If we regard the Lord's Supper as a mere memorial and nothing else, we cut ourselves off from the immediate benefit of receiving the very life and power of Jesus. The Eucharist is the sacrament of our encounter with Jesus, and through it His power brings healing to our whole being through His body and His blood.

A good example of communicating Christ's victory over evil through the Eucharist is found in the life and ministry of John of Kronstadt, a nineteenth-century priest in Russia. He was a man of prayer, and his chief contribution to the Russian church was in connection with the profound, mystical, living experience of the Eucharist. In the Orthodox church no one is allowed to take Communion until he has confessed his sins to the priest. Since, in a large congregation, this practice inhibits frequent Communion, Father Kronstadt introduced the unheard of practice of general vocal confession. It was, as George Fedotov wrote, "an impressive, even terrifying spectacle: Thousands of people shouting aloud their most secret sins and sobbing for forgiveness."[8] Kronstadt himself reported the unusual results of seeking forgiveness and coming to the healing power of Christ in the Eucharist:

> I marvel at the greatness and life-giving properties of the Holy Sacrament. An old woman who was spitting blood, and who had lost all strength, being unable to eat anything, after the communion of the Holy Sacrament, which I administered to her, began to recover on the same day from her illness. A young girl who was

---

[7]Ignatius, "Letters of Ignatius: Ephesians" in *Early Christian Fathers*, ed. Cyril C. Richardson (Philadelphia: Westminster Press, 1953), p. 93.
[8]George P. Fedotov, *A Treasury of Russian Spirituality* (Belmont, Mass.: Norland Publishing Co., 1975), vol. 2, p. 349.

almost dying, after the communion of the Holy Sacrament began to eat, drink, and speak; whilst before this she was almost in a state of unconsciousness, violently tossed about, and could neither eat nor drink anything. Glory to thy lifegiving and terrible mysteries, O Lord![9]

Father Francis MacNutt in his work *Healing* discusses the phenomenon of communicating Christ's power over evil in the contemporary church. His experience, and that of many others, is that a real communication of healing power occurs through the sacraments of anointing the sick, penance, and the Eucharist, while a fourth sacrament, Holy Orders, empowers the priest to heal. MacNutt shows the depth of the church's perception that healing can be communicated through the tools of the church in the following statement:

> The basic reason why healing is desperately needed in order to renew penance is precisely because *repentance is not usually sufficient to root out the evil that holds us down morally and spiritually*. The more I deal with penitents the more I see that most moral problems that people face have a large element of the involuntary in them. The alcoholic seldom has merely a problem of willpower; he may also have a deep need for inner healing and, possibly, for deliverance as well. When a person comes to confession we cannot always expect that absolving the confessed sin will solve the problem; we ordinarily need to deal with healing the whole man.[10]

The victory of Christ over evil has the effect of transforming man and his world. This transformation is primarily a transformation of the Christian community, the church, which in turn radiates the message of redemption and reconciliation to the entire created order. The church is, therefore, called to be the recipient of the redeeming work of Christ and to be the source for the redeeming presence of Christ in the world. Thus, Christ communicates Himself to the church, and the church communicates Christ to the world.

[9]Ibid., p. 372.
[10]Francis MacNutt, O.P., *Healing* (Notre Dame, Ind.: Ave Maria Press, 1974).

CONCLUSION

The essence of this chapter has been to stress the role of the corporate church as communicator of Christ to the world. In America, and among Protestants in particular, we usually think of one-to-one interpersonal communication or electronic mass communication. We seldom think in terms of the communication made by the mere presence of a group in society. This tendency needs correction, because it disregards the total impact a unified body can make on society. It needs particular attention in the church, because this one-sided view of communication tends to make one see the church as a collection of individuals rather than as the *body* of Christ. By returning to the more corporate sense of the church, our theology of communication takes on a new dimension, an added depth.

We have discussed three ways the church relates to the world, and each of these suggests a different manner of communication.

First, the church is *identified* with the world (i.e., the created order—the structures of life). This relationship is a redemptive one that communicates the presence of Christ to the structures of the world. Two points are to be kept in mind in respect to this relationship:

- The church and the world stand toward each other in a *reciprocal relationship*. Specifically, whether the church takes an indifferent, positive, or negative attitude toward the created order and structures of society makes a difference in what is communicated. The church in this sense exerts a powerful influence on the culture.

- The presence of the church in the world establishes an *unconscious communication*. What the church is eventually seeps into the very warp and woof of society and expresses itself in art, literature, music, and architecture.

Second, the church communicates to the world (i.e., the powers of evil) by being *against* the powers. In this sense the church is not of the spirit of the world. There are a number of ways the church can communicate her stance against the powers. These ways were mentioned:

- Evangelism: The church is called to fulfill the great commission, bringing people to a saving knowledge of Christ.

- The prophetic stance: The church *lives* what she teaches. By adopting an alternative lifestyle (one which is no slave to the powers) the church acts as salt and light in society.

- The catachetical method: By setting forth the way of death and the way of life the church instructs her members in the Christian lifestyle.

Third, the church is victorious over the world (i.e., powers and spiritual wickedness). This position is rooted in the cosmic redemption Christ has wrought. Because He has destroyed the powers of evil, man and the created order have been released from the power of sin and set free. This freedom is experienced in the church now, to a certain extent, but will be fully realized at the consummation. In the meantime the power of Christ's victory over sin is communicated to us in at least the following ways in the church:

- Preaching: The preaching of the church is more like an announcement than a mere explanation or moralistic statement. It has to do with the Good News and should be proclaimed as an event that has already occurred. The powers and all their influence have been decisively defeated in the death and resurrection of Christ.

- The Holy Spirit: In the ministry of the Holy Spirit through unction, confession, and the Eucharist, there is a special communication of Christ's power over sin to those who hear and receive the healing word in faith. The church, therefore, as the community of those being healed, goes into the world to provide healing in the power of the Holy Spirit.

12

THIRTEEN BIBLICAL PRINCIPLES FOR CHRISTIAN COMMUNICATORS

In the previous chapters, I have been setting forth the subject of communications within the framework of a biblical view of life. It is important for the Christian communicator to see his or her work within this context. We sometimes do our work without a sense of where it belongs in the whole scope of things. This leads to impartial views of what we are doing as well as to frequent discouragement and despair. In order to have a sense of the *meaning* of our work, we need to understand it with reference to Christ and to the meaning of life in general and of our life in particular, which flows from Him.

For that reason this chapter is a summary of the major biblical themes from which a Christian understanding of communications is derived. They are easy to remember and should provide a basis for further thought and discussion.

A CALL TO EFFECTIVE COMMUNICATION

1. The task of the church is to communicate Christ to the contemporary world.

   - The Christ we are called to communicate is the cosmic Christ, not a false, distorted, or partial Christ. He is the Second Adam: In and through Him, man and the created order have been re-created.

   - For this reason, the entire world of man—all his activities under the sun, all he seeks to create and shape—constitutes the parameter of Christian communication.

2. The *problem* of communicating Christ is defined as follows:

building bridges between Christ and the cultures of the world.

- Communication must be understood as a process. This process involves understanding the message in its original context, admitting our own cultural framework through which our perception is filtered, and realizing that our communication must pass through the receivers' grids.

3. The *issue* of Christian communication is the awakening of faith.

- We tend to communicate our own culturalized view of Christianity. For this reason we need to recover the biblical notion of faith. This involves a turning away from the rational, romantic, and irrational distortions of faith and recovering the correlations among faith, hearing, and living.
- Faith is expressed in terms of awareness and obedience. Awareness affects the mind and establishes a new perspective toward life. Obedience affects living and creates a new set of values, goals, and purposes.

A BIBLICAL BASIS FOR COMMUNICATION

4. The eternal point of reference for communications is in the Trinity.

- The ability to communicate reaches all the way back into God Himself. Our confession of God is triune. He is, always has been, and always will be in relationship to Himself. Thus communication is part of the very essence of God. He Himself establishes the principle of communication.

5. Communication in this world is grounded in God's act of creation.

- Creation is the out-working of God's inner self. Because communication is central to what God is, it lies at the heart of His created order as well.

- The Christian view of creation affirms that no reality exists outside of God, that He created the world freely from His thoughts, that the world is a reality in and of itself. For these reasons the images of God in the world are expressions of the nature of God.

6. God has communicated to the world through revelation. These forms are models for our methods of communication.

   - God's revelation is *historical*. Our communication must relate to the everyday occurrences, the trials and troubles of existence. It must be a message to man in the midst of his suffering, oppression, poverty, hunger, and need. It dare not be out of touch with life.

   - God communicates through *language*. In our own use of words we must preserve the language of essential Christianity, making sure that what we communicate is biblical truth. Nevertheless, we are free to exercise our imagination in the use of analogies and illustrations for the purpose of communicating the Christian message.

   - God communicates through *vision*. It is a recognizable fact that man finds his identity with the past through images, pictures, and ceremonies. We must recognize that man is not merely verbal but also visual and therefore seek to use the visual as a proper form of communication.

   - God communicates through *incarnation*. In the incarnation God set forth the ultimate standard of communication. If we would reach others as God reached us, we must be willing to identify with the very life, the social context, and the needs of those with whom we communicate.

7. Man is created in the image of God: Thus man is to project God's image in every respect, including in his ability to communicate.

   - The image of God in man cannot be limited to the religious aspect of man. It points to the very heart of what man is. Man is able, to a certain degree, to shape history and to determine the outcome of personal and world events because he is made in the image of God.

- When man is in fellowship and communication with God, all areas in which he functions as a communicating being are in balance.

8. The fall of man has drastically affected communication in every area of man's existence.

- *The breakdown of communication between man and God.* The break between man and God is spiritual, having consequences as well in the physical and material realm of man's life in the world.

- *The breakdown of communication with self.* All mankind is aware of the loss of the presence of God and, therefore, of their own incompleteness. Man does not know the true meaning of his existence and thus casts about for something or someone in whom to find meaning and security.

- *The breakdown of communication between man and man.* Because man is the agent of cultural unfolding, it is only natural that the whole sweep of human history reflects the character of man. Man unfolds culture in such a way that culture personifies and enlarges man's self-alienation.

- *The breakdown of communication between man and nature.* Creation does not belong to Satan, but it has become the arena in which he exercises his authority over man. It has become the domain and the instrument of Satan. In this sense the creation is also alienated from God, and man is alienated from the original purpose and meaning of the creation.

9. Christ is the new image of man: As the Second Adam He re-creates the old creation and makes all things new.

- The sin of the first man bore cosmic results, beginning a chain of events that destroyed man's relationship with the entire created order and thus breaking down communication. The righteous obedience of the Second Adam, however, reversed that order of events and brought potential healing to all those broken relationships.

10. The church is the locus of the new order. It is here, in the

church, where communion with God has been restored and where potential healing of the breakdown in communication is found.

- The doctrine of the atonement holds the key to the restoration of broken communication. Christ broke the power of evil that held sway over the lives of men and perpetuated the breakdown of communication in every area of life. Now man is no longer in bondage to sin but is free to live in genuine community with God and his fellow men in the life of the church.

- Christ's work and the church as an extension of Himself in the world repair and restore man's communication with God, himself, fellowman, and nature. Nevertheless, the restoration of communication is an ongoing process, not finally and ultimately complete until the consummation.

THE CHURCH AND COMMUNICATION TODAY

11. There is a need today to restore symbolic communication within the church. Rational discourse alone is inadequate in an age of imaginative and visual images.

   - The nature of faith itself demands the transformation of supernatural concepts into visible images and symbols. Because no finite language can fully and completely express supernatural truth adequately, biblical religion and the church in history has always relied on symbolism as a means of communicating that which transcends the realm of the finite. The language of faith has always, therefore, been a language of symbols.

12. There is a need today to restore the sense of the church as a nurturing community. The church, which is in inseparable union with the Holy Spirit, is the context in which growth in Christ is communicated.

   - Growing in Christ is not merely accumulating knowledge or adopting a moralistic set of rules; rather it is learning to unite with God by the Holy Spirit through Jesus Christ.

- The church is a nurturing community because in and through the church, as the body of Christ, the Holy Spirit works to mold the character of each member so that growth in Christ occurs.

13. The church communicates outside of herself to the world in three stances: She is part of the world; against the world; and victorious over the world.

- Because the church is a visible part of the world, and therefore inextricably interwoven not only with the physical and social environment but also, and more significantly, with the structure of meaning, the action of the church as a means of communicating the gospel is of real significance.

- God speaks through the church as she stands against the world (i.e., the powers of evil). In our time God is calling the church to stand in a forthright way as a community of people who will not be ruled by the powers.

- Because Christ is victorious over the world, the church, which is the body of Christ in the world, is called to exercise Christ's victory in the world now. Christ continues His presence in the world through the church by the power of the Holy Spirit. The church anticipates the consummation when the work of Christ will be completed and all things will be made whole.

CONCLUSION

My main purpose in this book has been to develop a theology of communication. As I have read and thought about this subject, I have become increasingly aware that a theology of communication is not a theoretical discipline alone. We are dealing not so much with something we ponder but with something we *do*. A theology of communication is not an abstraction. It is an *action*. It is based on the God who acts, the God who makes Himself known, the God who is willing to take the risk of becoming involved.

For this reason it is important for us to see communications from a theocentric basis. But unless we *do* something about the knowledge gained, it will be little more than an intellectual idea dropped here and there in conversation to prove our erudition.

The point is that *God still speaks*. He speaks through us to the world. We are the voice of God, the carriers of His message.

We live in a world that desperately needs to hear the message we bear. I hope the material of this book will be more than an intellectual exercise. May it be an incentive to action and an aid to becoming a more effective voice of God, not only by what we say but also by what we do. In this way, then, God still speaks. Let the earth hear His voice!

SELECTED BIBLIOGRAPHY

Alston, William P. *Philosophy of Language.* Englewood Cliffs: N.J., Prentice Hall, 1964.

Aulén, Gustav. *Christus Victor.* New York: Macmillan, 1961.

Baillie, John. *The Idea of Revelation in Recent Thought.* New York: Columbia University Press, 1956.

Barton, Bruce. *The Man Nobody Knows.* Indianapolis: The Bobbs-Merrill Co., Charter Books, 1962.

Beardslee, John W., III., ed. *Reformed Dogmatics.* New York: Oxford University Press, 1965.

Berkhouwer, Cornelius G. *Man: The Image of God.* Grand Rapids: Eerdmans, 1962.

Bettenson, Henry. *The Later Christian Fathers.* New York: Oxford University Press, 1972.

Bieler, André. *The Social Humanism of Calvin.* Richmond: John Knox Press, 1964.

Boman, Thorleif. *Hebrew Thought Compared With Greek.* Philadelphia: Westminster Press, 1960.

Brunner, Emil. *The Christian Doctrine of Creation and Redemption.* London: Lutterworth Press, 1952.

Carrington, Philip. *The Primitive Christian Catechism.* Cambridge: University Press, 1940.

Cooke, Bernard, S.J. *Christian Sacraments and Christian Personality.* New York: Doubleday, 1965.

Cullman, Oscar. *Christ and Time.* London, SCM Press, 1951.

Dix, Gregory Dom. *The Image and Likeness of God.* New York: Morehouse-Gorham Co., 1954.

Ellul, Jacques. *The Meaning of the City.* Grand Rapids: Eerdmans, 1970.

Engel, James F. *Contemporary Christian Communications.* Nashville: Thomas Nelson, 1979.

209

Fedotov, George P. *A Treasury of Russian Spirituality*. Belmont, Mass.: Norland Publishing Co., 1975.

Gillquist, Peter E. *The Physical Side of Being Spiritual*. Grand Rapids: Zondervan, 1979.

Hagglund, Bengt. *History of Theology*. St. Louis: Concordia, 1968.

Harnack, Adolf. *What Is Christianity?* New York: Harper & Row, 1957.

Hesselgrave, David. *Communicating Christ Cross-Culturally*. Grand Rapids: Zondervan, 1978.

Hippolytus. *The Apostolic Tradition*. Edited by Burton Scott Eaton. Harnden, Conn.: Archon Books, 1962.

Holmes, Arthur. *All Truth Is God's Truth*. Grand Rapids: Eerdmans, 1978.

_____. *Faith Seeks Understanding*. Grand Rapids: Eerdmans, 1971.

Hutter, Charles, ed. *Imagination and the Spirit*. Grand Rapids: Eerdmans, 1971.

Jackson, Benjamin Franklin, ed. *Communication: Learning for Churchmen*. Nashville: Abingdon Press, 1968.

Jones, Cheslyn; Wainwright, Geoffrey; and Yarnold, Edward, S.J., eds. *The Study of Liturgy*. New York: Oxford University Press, 1978.

Kaufman, Gordon D. *Systematic Theology*. New York: Scribner, 1969.

Kelly, J.N.D. *Early Christian Creeds*. 3rd ed. New York: David McKay Co., 1972.

Kraemer, Hendrick. *The Communication of the Christian Faith*. Philadelphia: Westminster Press, 1956.

Ladd, George Eldon. *The Presence of the Future*. Grand Rapids: Eerdmans, 1974.

MacNutt, Francis, O.P. *Healing*. Notre Dame, Ind.: Ave Maria Press, 1974.

Manschreck, Clyde L. *A History of Christianity*. Vol. 2. Englewood Cliffs, N.J.: Prentice-Hall, 1964.

Mavis, Curry W. *The Psychology of Christian Experience*. Grand Rapids: Zondervan, 1963.

McNulty, Edward. *Gadgets, Gimmicks and Grace*. St. Meinard, Ind.: Abbey Press, 1976.

Meyendorff, John. *Byzantine Theology*. New York: Fordham University Press, 1974.

_____. *St. Gregory Palamas and Orthodox Spirituality*. New York: St. Vladimir Seminary Press, 1974.

Mowrer, Hobart. *Learning Theory and Personality Dynamics*. New York: Ronald Press Co., 1950.

Nida, Eugene. *Message and Mission*. New York: Harper & Brothers, 1960.

Olson, Bruce. *For This Cross I'll Kill You*. Carol Stream, Ill.: Creation House, 1973.

Ong, Walter, S.J. *The Presence of the Word*. New Haven: Yale University Press, 1967.

Orr, James. *The Christian View of God and the World, as Centering in the Incarnation*. 3rd ed. Edinburgh: Andrew Elliott, 1897.

Pulkingham, W. Graham. *Gathered For Power*. New York: Morehouse-Barlow, 1972.

_____. *They Left Their Nets*. New York: Morehouse-Barlow, 1973.

Read, David, H.C. *The Communication of the Gospel*. London: SCM Press, 1972.

Richards, Lawrence, O., *A Theology of Christian Education*. Grand Rapids: Zondervan, 1975.

Richardson, Cyril. *Early Christian Fathers*. Philadelphia: Westminster Press, 1953.

Richardson, Don. *Peace Child*. Glendale, Calif.: Regal Books, 1974.

_____. *Lords of the Earth*. Glendale, Calif.: Regal Books, 1977.

Rogers, Carl R. *Client-Centered Therapy*. Boston: Houghton-Mifflin Co., 1951.

Sayers, Dorothy. *Mind of the Maker*. London: Religious Book Club, 1942.

Schmemann, Alexander. *Introduction to Liturgical Theology*. New York: St. Vladimir Press, 1975.

Schweitzer, Albert. *The Quest of the Historical Jesus*. New York: Macmillan, 1953.

Serno, Kenneth K. and Mortensen, David. *Foundation of Communication Theory*. New York: Harper & Row, 1970.

Stedman, Ray. *Body Life*. Glendale, Calif.: Regal Books, 1973.

Stott, John R.W. *Confess Your Sins: The Way of Reconciliation*. Philadelphia: Westminster Press, 1965.

_____. *Christ the Controversialist*. Downers Grove, Ill.: Inter-Varsity Press, 1970.

Stowe, Everett M. *Communicating Reality Through Symbols*. Philadelphia: Fortress Press, 1970.

Stringfellow, William. *An Ethic For Christians and Other Aliens in a Strange Land*. Waco, Texas: Word Books, 1973.

Webber, Robert. *Common Roots: A Call To Evangelical Maturity*. Grand Rapids: Zondervan, 1978.

——————. *The Secular Saint*. Grand Rapids: Zondervan, 1979.

Wolterstorff, Nicholas. *Reason Within the Bounds of Religion*. Grand Rapids: Eerdmans, 1976.

Wooldridge, Dean. *Mechanical Man: The Physical Basis of Intelligent Life*. New York: McGraw Hill, 1968.

Yoder, John Howard. *The Politics of Jesus*. Grand Rapids: Eerdmans, 1972.

INDEX

SCRIPTURE INDEX